D1551267

"PARDON ME,

YOUR MANNERS ARE SHOWING!"

Professional Etiquette, Protocol & Diplomacy

*"Life is not so short but that there
is always time enough for courtesy."*

-Ralph Waldo Emerson

Bruce Gjovig, Chair
UND Alumni IFC

© *1992 UND Alumnae Panhellenic Council*
UND Alumni Interfraternity Council

© *1992 UND Alumnae Panhellenic Council*
UND Alumni Interfraternity Council

All rights reserved. No part of this book may be reproduced or transmitted in any form or by any means, electronic or mechanical, including photocopying, recording or by any other information storage or retrieval system without permission in writing from the publisher.

Publisher: Center for Innovation & Business Development
Box 8103, UND Station
Grand Forks, ND 58202
Phone   (701) 777-3132
FAX   (701) 777-2339

Copies available for $10 each plus $3.00 for postage and handling. Bulk purchases are available for sales, promotion, or educational use. Contact the publisher for details.

Library of Congress Catalog Card Number: 92-90582

ISBN Number: 0-9626855-1-8

Printed in the United States of America

CONTENTS

ACKNOWLEDGEMENTS

This book resulted from strong encouragement by Greek alumni at the University of North Dakota who wanted undergraduates to feel comfortable in any social situation – dining with executives, introducing a sister to a dignitary, or aiding the family of a deceased friend. Acquiring professional etiquette, manners, and diplomacy while in college can propel graduates upward in their careers, heading for success. The idea for this book came from Wesley Christenson '64, President of Christenson & Company, a public relations consulting firm in Grand Forks, North Dakota. He is a chapter advisor to Sigma Alpha Epsilon. Marijo Loomis Shide '48, Past-President of the North Dakota Board of Higher Education, and International President of the General Federation of Women's Clubs, recognized the need immediately and focused our attention on Letitia Baldrige's *Complete Guide to Executive Manners*, our primary resource for manners in the 1990s. Ms. Shide is a member of Delta Delta Delta. Mae Marie Blackmore '47, Chair of the Alumnae Panhellenic Council, is our strongest champion for the publication, and is the senior editor. Ms. Blackmore is a member of Pi Beta Phi. To all of you, and others, who helped in so many ways, I say thank you!

– Bruce Gjovig, Chair
UND Alumni Interfraternity Council
(Delta Tau Delta)

FOREWORD

I'm impressed with *Pardon Me, Your Manners Are Showing* – not only because it is interesting and well-edited, but because it was done in the first place. It shows real leadership in the important world of fraternities and sororities, and should provide invaluable assistance to any college student fortunate enough to read it. The world has never been in greater need of a universal consideration for others. The flower children of the 1970's used to call manners "foppish," "elitist" and "archaic." They were wrong, because manners are <u>good human relationships</u>, and there is simply nothing more important than that. People with good manners know how to get along with others. They make others feel happy and secure. They know how to move through life with grace.

Sincerely,

Letitia Baldrige

ABOUT THE AUTHORS

Bruce Gjovig '74 is chair of the Alumni Interfraternity Council at the University of North Dakota, which works toward the growth and expansion of the Greek system. He serves as an advisor to Delta Tau Delta, and currently chairs the fund-raising efforts for the Delta Tau Delta Educational Foundation. He has raised over $800,000 since 1977 to assist chapter members with funds for academic scholarships, achievement awards, leadership programs, and special projects. He is the co-founder of the national educational foundation movement for college fraternities and sororities, which started at UND in 1977. More than 30 such foundations have been established across the country since then, raising millions of dollars to renovate or rebuild chapter houses, establish scholarship programs, and provide support for further personal growth of Greek members. He was named the Outstanding UND Greek Alumnus in 1990.

Mr. Gjovig is a manufacturing consultant and the founding director of the Center for Innovation and Business Development at UND. The Center has helped launch over 140 products and new manufacturing companies since its start in 1984. He is the author or editor of three books on business planning, market planning, and entrepreneurial ventures. Besides his professional and fraternity activities, he is involved in leadership positions in several cultural, civic, and educational organizations.

Letitia Baldrige wrote the primary sources on which this publication was based. She is world famous as an expert on manners. She has served as the social secretary to U.S. Ambassadors Clare Boothe Luce in Rome, and David Bruce in Paris. She was chief of staff for former First Lady Jacqueline Kennedy. In the business world, she has served as Tiffany & Co.'s first public relations director, and Burlington Industries' first consumer affairs director. Baldrige is the author of <u>Complete Guide to Executive Manners</u> and <u>The New Manners for the '90s</u> and eight other books.

ABOUT THE SENIOR EDITOR

Mae Marie Blackmore '47 is chair of the Alumnae Panhellenic Council at the University of North Dakota. She serves as Chair of the Pi Beta Phi House Corporation, and has been active as an alumna advisor for thirty years. Ms. Blackmore has been recognized as the Outstanding UND Greek Alumna three times. She has been active with state and national professional organizations dealing with children and education, and has served on numerous boards for community, civic, cultural, and human service organizations.

Ms. Blackmore is a faculty emeritus of the Center for Teaching and Learning at the University of North Dakota, and retired in 1990 as Director of the University Children's Center after 31 years of service. An Air Force widow, she returned to Grand Forks to raise her four children.

FRATERNITY/SORORITY ENDOWMENT

Mr. Gjovig and Ms. Blackmore are co-chairs of the UND Fraternity/Sorority Endowment within the UND Foundation. A three-year fund drive is under way to raise a $250,000 endowment from which the interest will be used to enhance and strengthen the Greek system at the University of North Dakota. All profits and royalties from this book will be donated to build that endowment. All contributions, no matter the size, are welcome, and they are tax deductible.

INTRODUCTION

The premise of this book is that professional etiquette, protocol, and diplomacy offer you another strategy to get to the top, and stay there. Not only are these stepping stones to success, but also for life-long happiness and harmony.

Professional etiquette, manners, and diplomacy create a strong personal presence that can propel an individual to success. Acquiring knowledge and a college degree are not enough in a competitive global economy. Proper business protocol helps determine the success or failure of not only individuals, but companies, as well. Good manners prepare people to work with people of high rank and diverse cultures. A positive outlook, getting along with people, customer relations, initiative, and patience are all qualities directly affecting job performance. Real manners and thoughtfulness are the basis of wonderful human relationships, set the tone, and govern the finest interactions at work, home, leisure, the supermarket, the baseball field, the airport or over the phone.

Letitia Baldrige kindly granted us permission to quote from her books with the comment, "Good luck with the project and remember that good manners make you feel good, they make others happier, and they make the world work better."

Ms. Baldrige authored several books including Letitia Baldrige's Complete Guide to Executive Manners and The New Manners for the '90s. These excellent books are the resources for this publication, and are well worth the investment. We will touch the basics and, hopefully, interest you to further explore the essentials of good manners in social situations.

In The New Manners for the '90s, Ms. Baldrige says:

> I have always believed that there is a difference between etiquette and manners – and never more so than now, as we enter the nineties. Etiquette is protocol, rules of behavior that you memorize and that rarely bend to encompass individual concerns and needs. Manners embrace socially acceptable behavior, of course, but also much more than that. They are an expression of how you treat others when you care about them, their self-esteem and their feelings. Manners are under your control, because they come from your heart. In a chaotic world, they can make order out of disorder and give you the power to bring pleasure into other people's lives.

In a free society, informal codes of conduct, not laws, are the means of achieving cooperation, harmony, and productivity. Voluntary observance of these codes of conduct is everywhere: house rules, sportsmanship, professional ethics, ritual oaths, religious commandments, patriotism, etc. These codes embrace qualities such as loyalty, morality, integrity, hard work, respect for neighbors, protocol, and other virtues that serve the common good. Civilized behavior is learned behavior, observing codes of conduct called etiquette, manners, and diplomacy.

Americans seem to be becoming more rude, irresponsible, and selfish. In some areas, streets, malls, supermarkets, sports arenas, and other public places are becoming jungles populated with savages, i.e. coarse people doing their own thing without regard for anyone else. People scream, rant obscenities, are abusive and violent, and have savage inclinations to rob, cheat, steal, tell lies, cut corners, vandalize, sue the neighbors, ignore responsibilities, and trample on the rights of others. Informal codes of conduct, and etiquette, have been rejected or abandoned by these people. The worst in people is being brought out, not the best. Our country is poorer for this trend, and our quality of life is declining.

Fraternities and sororities have a great opportunity and a responsibility to provide the leadership necessary to build more civil communities, better workplaces, and a "kinder and gentler" society. Greeks have a proud tradition of providing excellent social training to those who did not have an opportunity to gain etiquette and leadership skills in earlier years. These skills promote professional success as good communication skills, excellence, and quality are recognized. <u>This book will suggest solutions for dilemmas, answer difficult questions, serve as a guide to living with others, and help you become a professional</u>. We hope this information helps you become comfortable in any social situation, and makes you feel as good as you make others feel good. Good relationships don't just happen, they are the result of hard work and caring.

<u>The **cardinal rules** of etiquette and manners are thoughtfulness and kindness</u>. The people to whom you are closest warrant an extra measure of consideration. After all, they are a part of your daily life. If a chapter house is to be a home, sensitivity to others, caring and mutual respect will keep close relationships comfortable and warm. Friction and rudeness will sour common living space, just as it will in the family home. Treating others well, individually as well as a group, will be easier if you have developed good habits on a daily basis.

Etiquette and good manners are at their best when informal. The best manners are not stuffy or forced but come naturally and easily. They are a part of the person – a habit – not something just for special occasions. Manners cannot be turned off and on: they are part of your character. **Etiquette** is protocol to be used in prescribed situations. **Manners** are an expression of how you treat others; thus embrace socially acceptable behavior.

To begin this book on a crucial point of etiquette, the classic pronoun "he" denotes "any person" and is used to refer as much to a woman as it does a man. Unfortunately, there is no pronoun that covers both genders. So you can be spared the clumsy redundancy of reading both "he" and "she," only one pronoun is used.

In the following pages, important rules for social customs are discussed. Only the most common customs are included, and the reader should consult more comprehensive works on the subject for specific details. Also keep in mind that etiquette and protocol change very little over time, but good manners change as society changes.

1. SOCIAL INTRODUCTIONS

A. Order of Introductions, Proper Phrases

It is nice to be around a person who is adept at making introductions and being introduced, saying hello or goodbye. Everyone is made to feel comfortable in a social situation; and there are no strangers, just friends waiting to meet.

Precedence. Rules of precedence are not as rigid as they once were; but as general rules, men are introduced <u>to</u> women, a younger person <u>to</u> a more senior one, a peer in another group <u>to</u> a peer in your group, a nonofficial person to a person with a title or rank. (For example: Betty, this is my roommate, Brent Black; Brent, this is Betty Cooper. Professor Olson, <u>may I present you to</u> my mother, Mrs. Smith. Bishop Williams, may I present Mr. Berg, my uncle.) Note that the person being <u>presented</u> is mentioned second. When introducing two people with equal prominence, introduce the person whom you know less well to the person you know better, i.e. introduce a visitor to a colleague.

Introduce people by making each person sound – and feel – important and wonderful. Introductions are simple, direct, and dignified. Explain who the people are when you introduce them. For example: "Jill, I would like to introduce you to my brother, John. John, I would like you to meet the President of our chapter, Jill Peterson." It is appropriate, and always helpful, to add identifying remarks to give common ground for conversation. Use a firm, practiced handshake, neither bone-crushing nor fish-limp.

Using "Ms." The use of "Ms." is no longer controversial and it is here to stay. Ms. is equal to Mr. Today "Miss" is old fashioned and reserved for young women up to age eighteen. "Ms." is used in all written invitations and letters without thought of marital status. In introductions, it is easier for many people to say "Miss" rather than "Ms.," which can sound like a buzzing bee; so if you find yourself saying "Miss" in conversation, it is just fine.

You also have a responsibility to make it easy for other people to know how you should be introduced correctly. If you have a difficult name or title, or there's been a change in your name or title, let people know. Always send out a change of address or telephone number to everyone with whom you do business or communicate.

If seated before an introduction is to be made, rise to acknowledge the person and remain standing until other members of the party are introduced. If seated at a table and it would be inconvenient for other persons at the table, do not rise during an introduction. Do not rise when introduced to persons who are themselves seated at a table. When someone is introduced to you and you remain seated, you are telling that person, even if you don't mean to, that you do not wish to be bothered. Your body language denotes lack of interest.

Remember names. Concentration is the key to remembering names. Pay attention during an introduction, and repeat the name mentally and in your conversation. Associate the name with the person's looks and activities to help you recall the name later. For a woman who has kept her family name after marriage, make sure both names are said clearly. It is up to the woman in this situation to make it clear during introductions so people remember. People care more about their names than all other names in the world. There is nothing as endearing as having someone remember your name after you have only met once.

First names. If you have to stop and think about whether you should use a person's first name, don't. There is a right time and a wrong time to start calling people by their first names. As a general rule, anyone in their twenties addresses someone over forty as "Mr." or "Ms." In some parts of America – small towns and rural areas – everyone is automatically on a first-name basis, but this is rare. A younger person should wait for an older person, professional, or person of rank to ask him to call him by his first name. It is a question of understanding deference. In any formal setting, nicknames should not be used. Everyone has a right to be introduced in the most dignified way possible.

A forgotten name. When you start to introduce two people and your mind goes blank, you are facing the most frequent source of embarrassment in polite society. Apologize for the memory lapse, or ask the people to introduce themselves. Do not ignore the people as it will make them uncomfortable. Always be prepared to jump in offering your name to help in the event the person making introductions forgets your name. This is an act of mercy, and ensures that the person you are meeting knows your name. Forget the expression, "Do you remember me?" Do not chance embarrassing someone, or putting them on the spot. **Name tags** should be worn on the <u>right</u> shoulder as they are easier to read when shaking hands.

The way you greet others – what you do with your body and your voice – shows the kind of person you are. If you meet others with interest, showing good manners, they will respond immediately to you. **Remember, you never get a second chance to make a good first impression!** Kisses, hugs, and warm embraces are reserved for family and close friends we have not seen in a long time. Putting your hand over their hand or on a shoulder is an appropriate sign of warm affection in a professional setting. Be mindful that people do not like to be "pawed."

When being introduced, it is important to:

- **Rise**
- **Step forward, smile, keep eye contact**
- **Give your name if not offered**
- **Shake hands firmly**
- **Repeat the other person's name and say something like, "Hello, Mr. Smith" or "Delighted to meet you, Ms. Smith" or "Nice to meet you, Professor Smith."**

B. Parties and Rush Functions

It is important to socialize and **"work the crowd"** the entire time at a social function. Do not stand in the corner and just chat with your pals, enjoying the food and drinks. Do not leave the room to catch your favorite TV program or make calls to friends. Your absence is noticed and tells people you lack interest in them as guests. Every person in the host group should be there (meaning 100% participation), introducing newcomers and guests, making sure everyone has met each other, and welcoming everyone to your function. The idea of a party is to make contact with as many people as possible in a short period of time, making guests feel welcome.

Mix. The hosts, not the guests, have the primary responsibility to mix. Hold up your end. Introduce yourself to those who look alone or ill at ease. Make pleasant conversation for at least five minutes. The music should never be so loud people cannot visit . . . that is why they are there. Remember the social you attended and were **ignored**, and you vowed never to go through that torture again.

Keep good eye contact and listen to his story. Do not look over his shoulder or around the room to see if someone more important or interesting has arrived (a common rudeness). Do not monopolize celebrity guests, so that others cannot get near them.

Guests need to thank the hosts just before leaving. You should acknowledge every courtesy extended to you. Your sense of appreciation should be so sincere and responsive as to make it impossible for generous acts to go unrecognized. The last duty of a guest is to leave on time.

C. Handshakes

Many people feel they can "measure the worth" of another person by his handshake. A handshake is an important contact – a physical link – between two people. It is an American tradition. Europeans hug when they meet, the English nod, the Japanese bow, but Americans shake hands. It is an integral part of the impression you leave, and receive, from the other person.

Handshakes should be used when being introduced, when someone comes to your home or office, when entering a room of people, and when you leave a gathering.

A good handshake is made with a firm, full-handed grasp, neither bone-crushing nor fish-limp. Shake from the elbow, not the wrist or the shoulder, keeping good eye contact. Hold with a steady squeeze for about three seconds, with an understated down snap (but no up-and-down pumping), followed at once with a decisive release. Sounds easy enough, but rarely do you encounter a really good handshake. Between two people who have a special relationship, an extended grip with eye contact, sometimes the left hand on top of the right hand, is a show of warm affection.

Convention says that a man should wait for a woman to extend her hand before shaking hands. The grip is the same, but men need to be careful of squeezing fingers with rings. Men rise when shaking hands, and women should too in professional settings. If your hands tend to be clammy, carry a handkerchief to inconspicuously wipe them off at a social gathering. Carry drinks in the left hand to avoid having a cold, wet, clammy right hand. Apologize for a cold hand if you get caught. Always take the right glove off to shake hands. The only woman who keeps her gloves on is the Queen.

D. Alumni and Parents

When parents or alumni visit, they should be treated as special guests by you and your friends. Although alumni may be the "landlords" of your chapter house, they are still guests in your home. Doorbells should be answered promptly, and guests should be escorted into the living or sitting room. Introduce yourself, and always use "Mr.," "Mrs.," or "Ms." until they ask you to use their first names. Offer to hang up their coats and hats, and assist them with their belongings. Offer a beverage if available. You are their host until someone else assumes that role. Be sure to give them a warm farewell when they leave.

As any guest enters the room, everyone should stand, and promptly introduce themselves, offering information which may be helpful in general conversation. This may include hometown, major, upcoming events and activities, or your association with the person they came to visit. Keep it light and general. This is an opportunity to share pleasantries and accomplishments, not war stories. Personal details or inside jokes are not appropriate. Do not leave guests alone and unattended. Make them feel welcome, comfortable, and important.

Invite alumni and parents over for a meal (formal meals are best) or to attend a banquet or event where there is a guest speaker. Include important alumni in your activities. They can be great mentors, give you valuable insight into the professional world, offer advice on good operations, and provide an excellent opportunity to practice your manners and your networking skills. They want you to do well.

E. Distinguished Guests

Distinguished and special guests whom you would treat with honor include a chapter consultant, a professor, a university leader, a wedding couple, an international guest, a guest speaker, an out-of-town visitor, the elderly, someone with a distinguished career, elected or appointed officials, and people celebrating a promotion, graduation, anniversary, or birthday. They will remember you for treating them with special courtesy.

Addressing Guests Appropriately. Use official titles when talking to or introducing people, even if they no longer hold that position. People like – and have the right – to be addressed by their proper names and titles. It is painful to be called by an improper name or to see one's name misspelled. A Major in the Air Force does not want to be addressed as a "Captain" or "Mister." A Bishop does not like to be referred to as a "priest." A former Governor, President of a University, Mayor, Ambassador, or United States Senator still has the title and should not be introduced as a "mister" or "Ms."

It is difficult to keep up with it all, but it is important to do so. Each of us has a responsibility to care about addressing other people properly. When you are in a protocol quandary, there are several places to go for help. Check in an etiquette book such as Letitia Baldrige's *Complete Guide to the New Manners for the '90s*. She has charts and 24 pages of how to address military officers, government officials, the clergy, foreign dignitaries, diplomats, and foreign professionals. The library, U.S. Department of State Office of Protocol, United Nations Office of Protocol, a local military installation, or the Mayor's office can all be of assistance. Should you be granted an audience with the Pope or the President, spend some time in the library before you go.

Some people have a title at work (Sergeant Wood at the Police Station or Captain Green of the airline) that they generally do not use socially. At home or a party, they use "Mr." or "Ms." However some have had the position for a long time, and also carry the title with them away from work. It is their choice.

A visiting **guest of honor** deserves special attention and treatment. Here are some things to remember:

- The guest should be met at the airport by someone of high rank. Help carry the baggage, and be prepared to answer all questions about the visit.

- There should be welcoming flowers, a basket of fresh fruit, and/or a small box of chocolates waiting in the hotel room. A personal note of welcome from the chapter president should also be waiting. He is likely tired from traveling, so do not talk his ear off. Protect him from social introductions until he has had a chance to rest. Make the visit comfortable. Ask if you can be of any special assistance.

- The guest should be provided with a complete schedule of events, along with appropriate details (size and type of audience, time allotted for speech, formal or informal dress, etc.) and guest lists. Giving a mere list of names is useless. The list should contain names, titles, what they do, why they are important, and other interesting information. Guests deserve to be well briefed.

- Comfortable transportation should be provided at all times.

- Brief the members of the host group prior to the guest's arrival so that all may be prepared and knowledgeable.

- A VIP is escorted to each event, and should be carefully introduced. If a reception is given in his honor, he should stand in a receiving line with the hosts making proper introductions.

- A keynote speaker should be put on the program early when both the audience and the speaker are fresh.

- Inquire about speaker fees and expenses at the time of the invitation to be sure it is within your budget.

- In the event of a late cancellation, ask a substitute to speak because of his ability, indicating your respect and appreciation of him. Don't say, "We knew you would do it," or "we asked because it is so easy for you." It isn't easy for anyone.

Toasting. The guest of honor should be given a toast by the host. Usually the host will be the only one to rise at the table. In large gatherings, the host may ask all present to rise and join him in the toast. The guest of honor will respond with a toast of his own, thanking the hosts. If you can be amusing, so much the better, but be light, short, and give dignified comments about that person's best qualities. Pick up your wine glass (or water glass if you choose not to drink or that is all that is available), look at the person being toasted, raise your glass and nod, then sip from the glass of wine after the toast ends. A common response to a formal toast by attendees is, "Here, Here."

It is also nice to turn to your dinner partners separately, raising your glass and nodding, then sipping, at the conclusion of the toasts of the host and guest of honor. Short toasts to your partners are as simple as raising your glass and saying "Cheers," "Here's to you," "Salut," or "Skoal" (Scandinavian). Many fraternal societies include as a part of formal occasions a standard toast to a founder, hero, or martyr of the society. Attendees rise, join the toast, and respond with, "Here, Here."

2. TABLE ETIQUETTE

Since a person's behavior at the table signals sensitivity to other people, it is very important to do it correctly. People look favorably upon those who are graceful and at ease. Over meals, people are hired, promoted, entertained, admired, and receive marriage proposals. When done poorly, meals are embarrassing, uncomfortable, even disastrous, if not unappetizing. Probably more people are offended at the table than any other place. You need to know how to make others feel comfortable at the table, and how to eat quietly, neatly, without drawing any attention to yourself. Here are the basic rules of table etiquette.

A. Setting the Table

The main reason tables are set more informally today than in past generations is that very few people have domestic help. The world is more informal and everyone seems too busy to give much attention to the formal rituals of life. However, when you have guests, it is time to make the effort. When you go to an obvious effort to make things attractive and pleasant for those you have invited to your home, the event almost always takes off. People feel festive and pampered – and you become appreciated.

Place Cards. Place cards make sense when you have eight or more people coming to lunch or dinner. When dinner is ready and guests go to the table, the host or hostess may be occupied, or may be taking care of the finishing touches. The host may not be near the table at the moment some of the guests take their places. With place cards, people can see where they are supposed to sit without further direction. That is why place cards are efficient.

The nicest place cards are made of thick white stock, and may be thinly bordered in silver, gold, or a color. Place cards may be single cards meant to lie flat on the table, or they may be folded "tent" cards, which stand up on the table. The place card is set on top of a napkin placed in the middle of the plate, or above the forks at the upper left of the place setting, or leaning against the stem of a water or wine glass, or just above the middle of the plate. The cards are handwritten in black ink (by someone with a good hand or a calligrapher), or typed (jumbo type, please) for a business meal.

For an informal party of friends who know each other, all you need write on the place cards are first names. For an informal party when the guests don't know each other, use both names, so each guest can glance at his dinner partner's card if necessary. For a formal dinner party, such as a business dinner or a function for a foreign guest – or any meal at which there will be people of rank – use only the surnames on the cards. A person who has held political office, or a military officer, or someone who holds a high appointed office is called by that rank or title on the place card, regardless of whether he still holds that office or rank.

The Table Setting. The rules of table settings hinge upon what is logical and efficient. Since most of us are right-handed and reach for our glasses with our right hands, then it's logical to place all glasses in the upper right portion of the place setting. A table set for guests should contain:

- Centerpiece decoration, including new candles if your party is an evening one. (Candles are not appropriate for lunch.)

- Either a bare place, or a plate, ready to receive food, or your first course already served on a plate, with the following setting:

Diagram of Table Setting

Cups and saucers are shown by china company ads on the right-hand side of the place setting. That is incorrect. They place it there just to show the item to customers, which confuses many people into thinking it is supposed to be there from the beginning. It does go to the right; the key is NOT UNTIL coffee or tea is served following the meal. However, don't be surprised to find them at the table when you arrive, especially at large banquets.

Butter plates seem to be disappearing from tables in our weight-conscious society, but they are still used for formal meals. They are certainly the most efficient way to serve your guests rolls, breadsticks, or bread – or the items from a relish tray. Place it above the forks, to the upper left; place the butter knife horizontally across on the top, its blade facing inward. Have one or two small butter pats already in place on each butter plate, although you may pass around a small plate containing butter pats or butter balls and a butter knife for guests to help themselves. You would not use butter plates unless serving bread, muffins, popovers, or rolls, or a food requiring buttering – such as corn on the cob or baked potatoes.

If you don't own butter plates, always pass around a butter knife together with a porcelain dish containing pats of butter, a small container filled to the top with butter, or an elegant round container into which a plastic tub of margarine is slipped. Guests should each place the desired amount of butter on the side of the plate (not directly on the roll) and pass it on around the table to the right.

Salt and Pepper Shakers are placed either at the top center of each place setting or at the top, off to one side. If you don't have enough sets to supply each guest, set between every two place settings, or put them at angles to the centerpiece, so that four people can have access to one set. If you have only two sets, put one at each end of the table. Instead of salt shakers, you might come across a "saltcellar" in someone's home – a very small open receptacle for salt, with a tiny salt spoon lying beside it on the table. If there is no spoon, use the blade of your knife. Few people add salt to their food these days, which is a compliment to whomever prepared the food, as well as being more healthy.

While people are cutting down on their salt intake, they are not necessarily cutting down on the pepper. If you provide the table with a large **pepper mill** at each end, you will probably delight your guests, particularly if you are serving pasta. (The guests should use the pepper mill themselves; the host does not go around the table grinding pepper on food, like a waiter in a restaurant!) Salt and pepper shakers are passed <u>together</u>, one at a time, by the bottoms or sides. Fingers never touch the tops. Pass them to your right, keeping the set together to keep better track of them. Pepper mills can be passed independently of salt shakers, as they are not part of a set.

B. Entering the Room and Seating

Guests are escorted into the dining room first by their host (chapter president); women precede men. In the absence of place cards, guests sit to the right of their host, women to the right of men. If possible, a left-hander should be seated on the left end of the table – to make it as comfortable as possible for everyone. Gentlemen pull out chairs for women, slowly and carefully helping them move the chair forward. Men are seated after all the women are seated at the table. If there is just a table head, he sits first. Stand by your chair until guests and women are seated, sitting from the left side of the chair (your right side), unless obstructions prevent it. When there are many tables, guests should be seated at several tables, first to the right, then the left, of the table head.

Usually the chapter president or housemother is in charge of the dining room as a whole, with a table head at each table. These people are authorized, by their position, to admit or excuse people, call for service, interpret rules, make introductions, and insure compliance of good manners. At the chapter house, the order to enter and leave the dining room is (1) Housemother and escort (President), (2) special guests and escorts, (3) other guests and escorts, (4) initiated members, and (5) new members.

Do not remove your coat and hang it on the back of the chair. Coats are to be worn or hung in a cloakroom. Maintain good posture at the table, sitting erect but not stiff. You have options on what to do with your hands when not actually eating. You may prefer simply to rest them on the table (with the bottom of your <u>wrists</u> balanced on the table's edge), or you may prefer to leave your **hands** under the table in your lap. (Quiet hands look a lot better to others than hands playing with food on the plate or with strands of hair!) It is all right to rest an elbow or two on the table between courses, because that's a gesture that comes naturally to people engaged in animated conversation. While you are eating, though, it's best to keep **elbows** off the table. **Slouching** at the table is unattractive, and tipping one's chair is an unforgivable and most unfortunate bad habit. It looks sloppy, and is fatal to the back legs of the chair.

Often it is boring just to sit there waiting for people to finish their entree and their endless conversations, but keep those fingers from drumming nervously on the table or from playing with pieces of flatware or with the glasses. You may not hear the rat-a-tat-tat sounds, but it can annoy your neighbors.

C. Napkins

Napkins can be found in many appropriate places. Some hosts like to place the napkin in an empty water or wine glass, making a fan or a flower shape. The napkin may be folded and placed in the center of the plate. Or it may be folded imaginatively and tied with ribbon, or held together with napkin rings. The napkin in its traditional place is to the left of the forks. It looks best with the outside folds facing left, that is, the "corners" at the bottom right.

As soon as you sit down at the table, spread your napkin across your lap. Do not "snap" or wave it, but unfold it below the table. A luncheon-sized napkin (for example, 16 inches square) should be unfolded entirely, while a large dinner napkin (24 inches square) should be unfolded in half before placing it on your lap. Do not tuck it into your belt. The most important thing to remember about a napkin is that it should stay on your lap until you leave the table. If you must leave the table during the meal for any reason, put your napkin on the seat of your chair, not on the table. When people are eating, the sight of someone's soiled napkin tossed on the table is unappetizing. When it comes time to leave the table, fold your napkin (not necessarily neatly) and leave it on the table to the left of the plate. When the host lays his napkin on the table, it is a signal the meal is over.

Using the napkin as a bib. When you order a broiled lobster in a restaurant, the waiter might provide you with a bib to protect your clothing, but if not eating lobster, it looks pretty tacky to place a large napkin bib-style around your neck – except for children.

If you are eating a food that tends to spot clothing (i.e. soup, chili, barbecued ribs, spaghetti, or certain salads dripping in dressing), it's possible to protect yourself in a graceful way. Pull your chair in close and lean over the table when you eat this splashy kind of food. Take a corner of your napkin with the fingers of your left hand and hold it up to your throat, spreading the napkin loosely over your chest. Still holding the napkin against you with your left hand, eat the food with the fork in your right. If anything splatters, it will land on your napkin, not on your clothes – and other people will hardly notice that you are holding your napkin up to your neck.

A woman should not blot her **lipstick** on her napkin as it looks unattractive to others. A trip to the ladies' room before the meal to blot her lipstick with paper tissue is a much better idea – and much easier on the laundry operations.

The napkin should be used for the purpose it was intended – that is, the removal of particles of food or drink from the lips, and remotely to prevent food from staining one's clothing. To be used for more than a bare minimum of times in the course of a meal indicates a lack of grace and table manners. Blot or pat your lips, do not use the napkin as a washcloth.

Should you get something in your mouth which should not be eaten (**bone**, fruit seeds, olive pit, shell, etc.), quietly remove it with your fingers. Put it to one side of your plate. Never spit food out even if you don't like it. Painfully swallow it. Then leave it alone and keep quiet about it.

D. Serving Food

Food should be offered first to any honored guest or older person at the table. Pass the food first to the guests before helping yourself, and then it is passed **counter-clockwise** (to the right). When no guests are present, the head of the table is served first, then passed to the right. Any food on the table not already served is passed to the head for the first serving.

Food is passed to the right by reaching across your chest with your right hand (to avoid elbow clashes) to accept the item, place in your left hand, and serve yourself with your right hand. Then pass it to your right with your left hand, across the chest, with the handle of the container positioned for the receiver's convenience. Salt and pepper shakers are passed together, holding the sides or bottoms, never the tops. Fingers should never touch glasses, utensils, or any dinner items where they are brought to the mouth, or placed with food. It saves germs from being passed, and calms people who are sensitive to such things.

When serving yourself, take modest portions of food – even those items you love most like French fries, tacos, chili, and hot fudge sauce to ooze over your ice cream. If the food supply is plentiful, you can have **second helpings**, which pleases the host. It is far better to serve yourself a second time around than watch in horror because there is not enough for everyone because you have taken too much.

When waiters or waitresses serve. One person can handle a table of eight, but with ten or twelve guests to a table, it is more efficient to have two people serving. If two servers for your large table are not in the budget, go with one, but be content with having slow service. The waiter serves the food from the left side of the guest, and removes each **finished plate** from the right side of the guest, in the same direction food is passed. If a serving dish is hot, the waiter places a folded napkin under it to protect the palm of his hand. Beverages, of course, are served from the guest's right side, where the glasses are. (To serve the wine from the guest's left side would require reaching across the guest.) The proper way to remove a guest's finished plate is to remove it from the person's right with the right thumb clamped down on the fork and knife (or whatever implements are being used). In this way, the trip is made to the kitchen safely and gracefully. (No clattering from fallen plates and flying knives!)

E. Start of the Meal

"Please" and "thank you" are basic to good manners at the table. Rather than reach across the table to grab something, ask the person nearest to the item to "Please" pass it to you, and when you receive it, say a pleasant, "Thank you." You may be proud of your long reach in basketball, but if you use it at the dinner table to fetch something across the table, you might knock something over.

Grace may be said before the meal (which usually does not happen at dinner parties). Always follow your host's lead. He will either remain standing for the blessing of the food, in which case you should also, or the host will sit and announce that grace will be said. Don't eat or drink anything before grace has been said. Remain silent with your head bowed until the end, then put your napkin in your lap, and the meal will begin. Many chapters have a custom of "divine blessing" before meals, standing to sing a traditional song, taking their seats afterwards. Follow their lead. You do not have to make any gesture (Catholic sign of the cross for example) not practiced in your own faith. Guests occasionally may be invited to say grace and they should be alerted prior to coming to the table. So as not to be embarrassed by the request, know a short prayer such as, "For what we are about to receive, may the Lord make us truly thankful. Amen." or recite the family favorite.

The host, the guest of honor on the host's right, or the table head, should be the first to begin eating at the table. Everyone else will follow. If the food is cold, the host should wait until the last person has been served, not starting before the guests are ready. Wait even if the guest of honor has been engaged in animated chatter for what seems an eternity without picking up a knife and fork, leaving the rest of the guests at the table dying of hunger. At a large banquet, you may start eating when your table has been served, or those in your vicinity if seated at a long table. An exception to this rule is when the food on the table is hot. It is the responsibility of the host to urge the guests to begin eating at once, as soon as the food is served: "Please do start. Your soup will become cold, and it tastes so much better hot!"

F. Knife, Forks, and Spoons

Hold the knife, fork, and spoon with skill and dignity. Americans eat with the fork held in the right hand, tines up. Europeans eat with their left, tines down. Americans grasp the fork with the thumb and forefinger, about three-quarters of the way up the handle (not held in a fist). The thumb pushes against the back of the forefinger on top of the handle, and the other three fingers fit beneath the handle. The middle finger buttresses the handle from beneath. Hold your spoon the same way in the right hand. (Note: for left-handed people, the procedures described here are reversed, i.e. the European style.)

When you **cut** something requiring a **knife**, transfer your fork to your <u>left</u> hand and grasp it about two-thirds down the handle, tines down. (The American custom of "zigzag" eating calls for transferring the fork to the right hand for each bite, although it is okay to use the simpler European method by leaving the fork in your left hand.) The thumb and forefinger work together, the thumb applying pressure from the bottom. The forefinger, applying pressure from the top, stays a little closer to the fork tines than the thumb. This way, you can wield the fork to the left and to the right, still maintaining a firm grip and making the implement do what you want it to do. The knife is held in the right hand with the thumb and middle finger (grasping it halfway down the handle), and with the forefinger pressing down firmly on the top of the blade at the point where it joins the handle.

When **cutting**, keep your **elbows** as close to your body as possible, so your neighbor won't have your elbow in the ribs. <u>Cut your meat one small piece at a time</u>, eating that piece before cutting another. As a child, your parents may have cut up your entire piece of meat for you in small bites, but this is not for adults. Observing young people on college campuses and in the workplace, many of them hold their forks in their hand, making pugnacious **fists** while they draw their knives inefficiently across the meat, as if drawing a bow across a cello! Nor should you use your fork as a shovel. It looks clumsy.

Using the left hand, the knife can be used to **push** food onto the fork, the tip of the blade guiding the food onto the fork. A piece of bread crust may also be used. You may be surprised to find out this is correct, but it does save peas from rolling over the edge of the plate and across the table. Use your knife with your **salad**, if the pieces are too large. Better to cut a salad in small pieces than have a plant hanging from your mouth.

When you **pause** in eating your food, American-style, your knife (blade turned inward) rests on the upper right side of your plate. Rest your fork, tines up, parallel to, and below, the knife. Position your implements with the tines below the blade in the center of the plate (handles at the 4 o'clock position) when you have **finished** your meal. They are then ready to be removed (from the right, right thumb on the utensils). Once used, forks and knives rest entirely on the plate (no handles on the table, gang-plank style).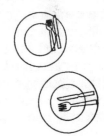

A **spoon** is meant to be laid to rest on a saucer, not left sticking up in a cup or glass or back on the table. (The soup spoon does, however, rest on the edge of the soup plate.) If you are served a tall glass of iced tea with a tall spoon or stirrer, balance this implement on the undersaucer when not in use. When there is no saucer, the stirrer remains upright in the glass. Be sure to grasp it between your index and middle finger while you drink so that it does not fall out. With soups or desserts, the spoon is dipped <u>away</u> from you. Then sip from the side of the spoon noiselessly. Do not blow on foods to cool them: just wait. If the last portion of soup is irresistible, tip the bowl <u>away</u> from you.

The right flatware. It is not uncommon to sit down at a formal dinner table and confront an array of eating utensils, all lined up in battle formation (see page 8). Panic may ensue, the guest wondering which to use for what. It is easy to make a classic error, such as using a spoon to eat the stuffed avocado during the first course instead of the tiny fork on the far right. The result is that when the creamy dessert is served, only a tiny fork is left with which to eat dessert. To make matters far worse, everyone at the table may follow your lead, thinking you knew what you were doing. In this case, ask the waiter to bring spoons for the entire table.

The table is set so that you <u>eat from the outside in</u>. In other words, you take the outside utensil for the first course, and then proceed, course by course, selecting the next utensil toward the plate until finally you have used them all. When in doubt, follow the leader (host, table head, or guest of honor), and if by chance you made an inadvertent mistake, ask for the proper implement. No harm is done other than wounding your pride.

Dessert utensils may either be set at the top of the place setting, or the dessert spoon may be placed on the inside right of the place setting. The waiter may bring you a plate with the proper utensils on it when dessert is served. If you set your table with the dessert implements lying horizontally at the top of your plate, put the spoon on top, bowl pointing left, and the fork beneath with tines pointing right. By the way, it's not necessary to use two implements for the dessert course. It just makes eating a little easier if there is something to help push the dessert onto the fork or spoon.

G. Bread and Butter

With a basket of rolls, bread or breadsticks adjacent to your place setting, offer a roll to the person to your left, then help yourself, and pass it to the person on your right...who will pass it on. If you have a **butter plate** (see also page 8), keep your roll there. Otherwise keep the roll on the left side of the plate. A roll should be pulled apart with the fingers into a bite size piece. It should not be cut with a knife. Don't "butter ahead"; rather butter each piece as you eat it. Keep the crumbs on the plate as much as possible. Pick up crumbs with your fingers, and put them on the plate. It can be done naturally during conversation so no one will notice you doing it.

Muffins or toast should be cut in at least halves with a knife, each portion buttered separately and then eaten, perhaps spread with some jam. **A hot popover** should be opened, then buttered in small pieces immediately. Once it deflates and cools, it loses its charm. **Sticky buns or Danish rolls** should be cut in halves or quarters with a knife, and then buttered. **English muffins** are already halved and toasted when served. If desired, spread the entire half with honey or jam with a knife, and eat from the half. **French bread** should be torn apart from the loaf, holding the loaf with the napkin on the outside. Pull apart pieces with your fingers and butter each piece as you eat it.

H. Dining "Faux Pas"

Although the positive approach to good manners is preferred, there are some table etiquette "faux pas" (French for "false steps") that are common, and should be brought to your attention:

Don't **push your plate** back when finished, or stack dishes. Leave them exactly where they are until removed by the waiter, or by yourself. Do not place or encircle your arm around the plate. No one is going to steal your food. Don't announce that you are "through" or "stuffed"; placing your knife and fork handles in the 4 o'clock position on the right side of the plate with the tines below the blade is signal enough (see page 13).

Don't take a drink if there is food in your mouth. Swallow first. Always chew with your mouth closed. Don't try to talk with food in your mouth; swallow first.

Don't wave a spoon or fork with food on it during conversation. Eat in small bites, and only one bite on a utensil at a time. Often you see people eat ice cream with several bites at a time on the spoon. Wrong.

Don't cut up your meat before you start to eat. Cut one bite at a time. Don't mix and pile food on your fork. Eat foods separately, and never take huge mouthfuls at a time.

Don't share food by spearing it with your fork and passing your fork. Instead, the receiver passes his butter plate, or main plate, and requests that a little of the food be put on it.

Women should never wear an excessive amount of **lipstick** to the table. It looks unattractive on the rim of the glass, on silver, or on the napkin. Blot your lips before entering the dining room. Consider your host.

Do not **smoke** while others are eating to avoid ruining the smell and taste of good food. Ask if you may smoke should there be those present who are allergic to smoke. Dangling cigarettes are very unattractive as are those waved about in conversation.

Never **groom** at the table. A woman can get by with quickly putting on a little lipstick, but even that is best done in the ladies' room. Never comb your hair at the table, or put your hands to your hair in any place where food is served.

Table hopping is not in good taste at a restaurant, and do not stop at tables and carry on long conversations. A simple "hello" to someone you know suffices. There are rare occasions when one or two introductions are suitable. All men at a <u>small</u> table (those in close proximity otherwise) rise when a woman is being introduced, women remain seated. Men do not rise for other men, except for the man being greeted, and then only for the handshake.

Never use a **toothpick** at the table, even if you feel you have a large wedge between your teeth. Try drinking some water to help the situation, and if you feel your teeth are really decorated with food, excuse yourself for a second to go to the restroom. There you can vigorously rinse your mouth – or even use your toothpick.

Disposing of toothpicks. At cocktail parties toothpicks don't just disappear, although guests wish they would. When you take a shrimp on a toothpick and dip it into a sauce, don't put the used toothpick back on the platter, because it certainly isn't appetizing for someone else who wants shrimp. When using toothpicks (and many refuse to serve hors d'oeuvres requiring them because of the hassle they create) provide containers throughout the cocktail area, so people can easily dispense with them. If you aren't using a small plate and there isn't an ashtray, a dish, or a wastebasket nearby, put used toothpicks in your cocktail napkin and then leave them in the kitchen or in a bathroom wastebasket before you leave.

I. Dinner Conversation

With TV, VCRs, computers, Walkman earphones, and other forms of passive entertainment and education, the art of good conversation between people is being lost. With all these electronics, the harmonious human voice engaged in pleasant conversation gives us a warm human touch we all need. However, no one needs a bore. A good conversationalist makes others feel good, stimulates our curiosity, and is a magnet to make people happy. **Remember, you were invited for your conversation, not your appetite.**

There is one sin of table etiquette that is unforgivable: **DO NOT TALK WITH FOOD IN YOUR MOUTH, OR CHEW WITH YOUR MOUTH OPEN.** You may consider that two rules, but if you break them, everything else you do won't matter. You will be branded as a crude dinner guest, no matter how well you handle the utensils. Learn to eat small bites to facilitate a smoother flow of conversation.

You are primarily responsible for talking to the people next to you at the dinner table. Know how to make small talk with people who are strangers, even those you are not fond of. The art of making good <u>business</u> conversation includes the ability to pass the time of day in agreeable conversation, by talking about various subjects while waiting for more substantial discussions to begin.

Engaging in intelligent conversation requires a broad familiarity with news, current events, literature, and entertainment. A liberal arts education suggests you have that ability. To keep up, read a daily newspaper, read a weekly news magazine, listen to the news, and be prepared to make observations on events and issues. Controversial subjects on politics, religion, sex, and money are off-limits except with close friends. Being a good conversationalist is a great asset, and anyone can be with practice. The use of slang or profanity is out of place in professional and polite society. Profane language shows lack of self-control, decency, and maturity.

Give equal time to everyone around you, even if one is more amusing than the others. If conversation bogs down, get the other person to talk about himself – hometown, trips, hobbies, projects, family, etc. Launch pleasant, positive, upbeat topics of conversation, human interest stories, and funny happenings; but not depressing stories. No one wants to hear about auto accidents, illness, depressing failures, raging opinions, critical reviews, etc. It is inappropriate to ask someone if it's true his brother has AIDS, if he just broke up, or why he got fired. The other person wants to enjoy himself, no matter how curious you are.

A good conversationalist is sensitive to the group and the occasion before leading the group. A funny off-color joke in the locker room is a sack of bricks in mixed company. Frivolous gossip at a funeral is inappropriate. Do not talk about golf when you are the only one who plays. Be interesting and thoughtful. Include new arrivals in the conversation by briefly summarizing the topic of conversation.

Be aware of times not to make small talk. Remain **silent** when someone is concentrating, working, reading, praying, or is intensely involved in something. Leave them alone. When riding in a car or airplane, be mindful that another person may not want to chit-chat. Should you be bothered by a "talker," be pleasant but firm: "I wish I could talk to you. I see you are an interesting person, but unfortunately I'm on a deadline and have a great deal of work to do before we arrive. I hope you don't mind."

You are a **bore** if their eyes glaze over, if they sink into the couch until they are nearly asleep, if they are glancing at their watch, or they gave up trying to interrupt you. The topics most likely to bore people are your job, family, illness, or gossip. Give only brief reports on these subjects, if asked, and veer to other topics. The bore is the epitome of the self-centered, and you can imagine him saying, "Enough of me talking about me. What do you think about me?" Let someone relate an important event which has happened without trying to top it with a story of your own. Let them have the stage.

Responding to the **conversational dilemma** takes talent. Bring up a new subject of conversation when:

- Stories are getting off-color, leaving others uncomfortable. Change subjects by asking someone in the group a question.

- People make mincemeat out of a friend who is not present to defend herself. Say, "Let's stop attacking Susan and attack the hors d'oeuvres instead."

- Technical jargon prevails, such as between computer enthusiasts; turn the conversation to current events.

- Someone has committed a gross gaffe (such as an ethnic joke before someone of that minority). Chilling quiet and stillness may follow. Break the silence with, "Well, I'm sure there will be apologies later, but for now, Terry just returned from Russia, and I would like to hear about her trip." Hopefully that person picks up the ball and starts to talk to dissipate the tension. The person who makes the error should take the offended person aside and make the most earnest of **apologies.** A <u>written</u> letter of apology should follow.

- Someone asks a personal or private question. Intervene immediately. If they still pry, put them in their place firmly. If someone asks if it's true someone is gay, say, "I suggest you ask him if you are that curious about his private life." If someone asks a single person if they are sleeping with someone, ask, "Why do you want to know; need a roommate?" It is alright to challenge an interrogator with, "I can't believe that <u>you</u>, of all people, would ask a question like that," or "I can't imagine a friend delving into such private matters," or "How would you feel if I asked <u>you</u> a question like that?" or "I'd rather not talk about that, if you don't mind," then change the subject.

- Someone says something rude or insensitive. You can say, "<u>Excuse me</u>," (with emphasis) "I don't think I heard you correctly." That gives the other person an opportunity to retreat or rephrase, catching his error. Many people do not mean to say many of the insensitive things they do.

Good conversation is pleasant and kind, and has the give and take on subjects of mutual interest. People like people who are upbeat, amusing, or informative. They make us smile. Remember to keep good eye contact when you are visiting, both when talking and listening. Give your undivided attention, and do not look at who else is in the room. Don't send a message of indifference or boredom. Excuse yourself politely if the need arises.

J. Tipping

The word "tips" originally came from the abbreviation for "to insure proper service." If you received proper service, you left a good tip. If you received poor service, you left a poor tip.

Some people feel that their moral obligation to tip ceases entirely when the service is rendered in an irritable, sloppy or inefficient manner. Tip a great deal less when service is rendered in a negative way, but remember many people rely on their tips for the major part of their income. To deprive them of every cent may be a real hardship. Give an unpleasant person a small tip of at least 5% just in case that person recently lost a spouse, or found out the bank account is hopelessly overdrawn, or that the children are in trouble at school. Maybe you were treated so badly because it was the worst day of his life and he still had to work.

When you are dining in a **fine restaurant**, tip:

- 20% of the bill, minus wine and taxes, to the waiter (75% of this tip goes to the waiter and 25% to the captain)

- 8% of the cost of the wines to the sommelier (wine steward); a minimum of $5

- $1 to the restroom attendant ($2 if they do something special for you like lending a sewing kit, finding safety pins, brushing you off, and the like)

- $10 to the maitre d', if he gave you a particularly good table or tried hard to please you

- $1 per coat to the coat check person ($2 if you left tote bags, briefcase, dripping umbrella, etc. in addition to a coat)

- $2 - $5 to the doorman for getting you a taxi (depending on how difficult it was to get)

- $3 to the valet parker for bringing your car around

When you are a host in a **modest restaurant**, there are fewer people to tip:

- 15% of the total bill, including wine, to the waiter

- $1 per coat to the coat check person

How you treat those who serve you is as important as the size of your tip. Big spenders and lavish tippers can be positively rude, treating people as chattel, ordering them about in loud, arrogant tones. Show dignity and respect for a person's job, and when you express your thanks with a compliment, it means more than a handful of dollars condescendingly proffered by a rude, mean person. Everyone in the service industry deserves nothing less than your recognition and sincere appreciation. Remember that superior service deserves commendation to management. A letter of appreciation, or a genuine comment, is most appropriate.

At a large private party, usually the only person who needs tipping is the valet parker who finds your car for you. Inquire first if the host has taken care of tips, and if he has, do not add another one. If not, give the parker $2 in a large city, $1 in a smaller one.

For a commercial **limousine**, in a large city, tip 20 percent of the bill; in a smaller one, tip 15 percent. The easiest way to handle this is to tell the limo service driver to add the proper percentage tip to your bill.

In a **taxi,** in a city like New York, you should pay a minimum of fifty cents tip for a ride. For a $5 ride, tip $1. For a $10 ride, tip $1.50 to $2. For a long ride, such as out to the airport, you would pay 15-20 percent of the total in tip. (If the driver really helps you with your baggage, other than just lifting it into his trunk – this is in the category of a small miracle – you would tip more, after you have recovered from the shock.) In a place like Washington, D.C., where drivers are paid on a confusing zone system, you usually tip the shorter rides up to the next dollar. For example, if your bill is $3.60, you would pay $4, if your bill is $4.50, you would pay $5. When your bill goes a lot higher, you would tip up to 15 percent of the fare.

Fast Food deliverers also deserve a tip, even if you are not obligated to do so. Give $1 for each box of pizza, and for oversized or several pizzas for a party, tip $5. Large quantities are hard to handle, and a tip makes the job easier . . . and you will be remembered for your courtesy and kindness.

Compliments are a way to let people know about the nice thoughts and feelings we have inside.

K. Thanking the Host

Before leaving, always thank the hostess and host for their hospitality. Always render appropriate acknowledgements for every courtesy extended to you. Every generous act deserves to be recognized. As a rule, obligations may be satisfied with personal thanks, a letter of appreciation, and if special courtesies were offered, by sending flowers, candy or a book, or by offering the same or similar courtesy – something of equal enjoyment.

Few people give compliments as often as they should, even if we all feel terrific when we get them. You don't have to lie and say you like something when you don't, but always find something redeeming and positive, and then comment on it. Look for opportunities to give a compliment such as:

- When someone is wearing new clothes
- After you have been served a delicious meal
- After someone has made a speech
- After someone has been recognized or honored
- When someone has made a great effort on a project
- When someone was courageous (sticking up for a friend)
- When someone won in competition

When someone compliments you, be a good receiver. How many times have you heard someone being paid a compliment and the receiver protests rather than say thank you. When someone says something nice to you, say, "Why, thank you!" or "Aren't you nice to say that!" or "I really appreciate those warm words." Don't put the other person down for saying something nice about you.

3. TELEPHONE ETIQUETTE

The general rules of etiquette to cultivate professional telephone manners are:

- Place your own calls
- Do not put people on endless hold
- Do not take telephone calls when someone is with you
- When calling a busy person, be sensitive about that person's time pressures
- Apologize for dialing a wrong number
- Identify yourself immediately when placing a call or answering
- The caller should make the first move to say goodbye
- When transferring a call, give the correct extension number in case the call is disconnected

A. Prompt Answers

Prompt answers are important. The phone should be answered within four rings. If the caller has to wait for ten rings or more, it appears the group is loathe to answer calls at all. All too many times, a phone rings forever where a group lives together, everyone expecting someone else to pick up the phone. The caller becomes frustrated, and thinks poorly of people who would let the phone ring while they are lounging, watching TV, and being generally inconsiderate. Be nice to the caller (even a stranger on the telephone), so that someone else is nice back to you. Suddenly two people feel better about themselves, spreading their good feelings.

Make good telephone answering a priority at the chapter house. The manner in which your telephone is answered says a lot about your concern for others and determines how you are perceived. In other words, your telephone manners will be judged by the way others in your chapter treat your caller. Birds of a feather . . . Asking someone to hold because another line is ringing is irritating, although it may also be unavoidable. In any event, the first call should take priority.

When answering the phone, your voice should sound warm, cheerful, upbeat, happy to be talking to the other voice – "Joe, it's great to talk to you! I've been thinking about you. We were wondering how you are." Do not use the cold and detached "Hello, Joe. What's up?" How you sound affects how people see you. Cheerful voices give a lift to the caller, for pleasant voices are contagious. Put a smile in your voice, and say "Hello" as though you are glad the telephone rang (although the effort is great if the call forced you out of the bathtub, and the person is selling magazine subscriptions).

In addition to the factor of warmth, a good telephone voice has:

- Clear diction (every sound is easily understandable)

- Normal tempo (the words do not tumble out too quickly or drag interminably)

- Pleasant volume (the caller does not speak too close to or too far from the mouthpiece, so one does not have to ask, "Would you please repeat that? Sorry, what did you say?")

- A good pitch (not too high and shrill, or gutturally low)

A speech teacher who works for a telephone company said she likes helping people change from "sounding either like a hog-caller or a baritone singing after ten beers" to a pleasant voice that is easy to listen to.

Write down exactly how you want the telephone answered. Post a script on the wall by the telephone, beginning with a bright, enthusiastic "Hello!" – and not a loud "Yeah?" Be sure to keep a notepad and sharpened pencil near every telephone in the house, so that lack of writing materials can never be an excuse for not taking a good message. (Store a large supply of pads and pencils. They last about two days by the telephone, after which one finds them under sofas, beds, and in dresser drawers.) If the person called is not home, the caller should be told promptly: <u>never</u> leave them on **hold** indefinitely.

Call when it's convenient for the other person, not just for you. Start the conversation with: "Is this a good time for you to talk?" Some people prefer to handle personal matters in the evening at home, others early in the morning before going to work. A caller should always be sensitive to the time pressures on the one you are trying to reach. By asking an important person's secretary when the best time is to call, you receive invaluable information.

B. Identify the Chapter and Yourself

Your chapter telephone, like a business phone, is properly answered informatively. It may be answered in this manner:

- "Delta Gamma, Joan Jackson speaking," or

- "Good Afternoon, Delta Tau Delta, this is Brad Cole, how may I help you?"

- When answering someone else's phone at their request, always identify the occupant, such as "Mary Smith's room, Pam Hagen speaking."

- When calling, also identify yourself, "Hello, this is Chad Black. Is Barb Olson available?"

C. Messages

Take accurate telephone messages for your housemates, and <u>make sure</u> you leave them where the person to whom they are directed can see them the minute he or she comes home. Return telephone calls within twenty-four hours, or have someone else handle the matter. It is good manners and good business to do this.

People should take accurate, legible messages for each other. It is an act of courtesy, and you would want the same done for you. The caller should not "overload" when leaving a message. A message should be uncomplicated including the caller's name, telephone number, the time of the call, the name of the person to whom the message is directed, and one simple piece of information or instructions. Repeat the telephone number to the caller to be sure you did not make a mistake, and ask the person to spell his name if you have any doubt. Sign your name to the message in case further clarification is necessary.

If you leave a message with if's, and's, and but's, you can almost be certain that it will not be transmitted with perfect accuracy. (The exception, of course, is a competent secretary, who can take the most complicated of messages perfectly. In fact, if you need assistance, ask the executive secretary!)

When reaching an **answering machine**, remember your objective was to reach the person, and this thoughtful person has a device that will register your attempt. Talk distinctly, speak slowly when you come to numbers, difficult names, or addresses. Give your name, the date, and the hour of your message. Come to the point of your message quickly. Say "Goodbye" in an up voice. If you sign off without one word, the other person may think you were cut off. Say something nice too before you sign off – such as "Hope all is well with you, John. Good-bye." Also be sure you have reached the right answering machine.

Your incoming and outgoing messages on an answering machine should be short, direct, and businesslike. Avoid the temptation to be funny and cute. Grandparents, and potential employers, may not be amused with oblique creativeness. My God, what might you say to a customer at work?

D. Other Good Telephone Etiquette

Unless you are absolutely, 100% certain of another's schedule, call only between the hours of 9:00 a.m. and 10:00 p.m. Do not call during meal times. We all deserve a break from the telephone. Always ask if this is a good time to visit. It may not be convenient because he is busy with work, company, cooking, feeding babies, family squabbles, or emergencies. Never end a relationship over the phone. It is the easy way, but the cowardly way. After five minutes, the caller should make a move to end the call, and do so unless invited to continue the conservation.

A. Hospitality Duties of the Host

Good manners in today's world are a larger part of our civilized society than most would possibly realize. Remember, real manners are instinctive; they stem from your character and your heart. You can't turn them on and off like a light switch. They are genuine, because you care about the dignity, welfare, and feelings of others. The people who are so nice to be around:

- are consummate hosts

- are engrossing guests

- have good table manners

- never mooch: returning hospitality, gifts, dinner invitations, and kindnesses of any kind – without ever demanding that anyone return their kindnesses

- use correct grammar and have a graceful vocabulary

- are excellent communicators – who make telephone calls, write letters, are in touch with people, instead of expecting everyone else to communicate with him

- seek out the wallflowers at a social event to bring them into the group

- rise to defend anyone who is unfairly criticized

Don't be a "dinner guest hog," which means that your friends are the ones regularly inviting you to have dinner. Ask if others would like to have one or two of their friends at the next party at your house. In other words, divide the opportunity for entertaining friends. But if your close friends don't seem to have anyone to suggest, just go ahead with your guests. Your roommates may prefer it that way. (Just be sure they do!)

Know how to talk to and help act as a parent's co-host. For example, when a father has come to see his daughter, shake his hand and say with a smile, "Hello, Mr. Gray. I'm Julie, nice to see you again. Here, I'll put your coat in the closet." "Thank you, Julie, nice to see you again." "Your daughter will be down right away. Would you like to sit down in the living room?" She then shows him into the living room and turns on some more light in the room to make it more cheerful. Offer refreshments if available. Alert the daughter her father has arrived. With this, Julie has done her duty and made the guest comfortable. She may now leave, unless she wishes to stay and chat until the daughter arrives, which is even more hospitable.

B. Entertainment Planning

The art of entertaining well is one of a person's greatest assets, and it should be used as part of your repertoire for making friends. Set up a "party notebook" – your manual – into which every pertinent item will be entered, from the budget to the invitation list, and from the kind of decorations to be purchased, to the number of lemons and limes needed for refreshments. Make a budget – always the next step – and if your means are limited, resolve to stick to it. Set your party date – one that will not conflict with a big social event or on a night when everyone wants to be home watching television (for example, Academy Awards night or a sports championship).

Decide on the type of party you want to give, the place and the hours for your party. Enter in the book the best guest list you can draw up. Invitations (R.S.V.P.) should be noted in your book. Keep an updated guest list in your party book, with the latest tally of acceptances and regrets so that you'll know exactly where you stand with your number of guests. Hire a caterer and/or the extra help needed for a large event, whether the extra help consists of a cook, bartender, babysitter, clean-up squad, or someone to mow the lawn so the guests don't have to wade through your ankle-deep grass.

Decide on your menu, list everything needed for the party, order in advance everything you can – well ahead of time. Pick your table decorations, entertainment, etc.

C. Being a Guest

The first rule is, if you can't say something nice, don't say anything at all, or stay home. Respect means not tracking in mud onto the floors, not putting feet up on a table or on the arms of the sofa, not getting food on the carpet. Timeliness and cleanliness are two virtues needed for a guest. On entering a home or chapter house, the first duty is to seek out the host and pay respects. After greeting the host, exchange greetings and mix and converse with other members of the group. It indicates lack of poise to detach oneself from the others at the first opportunity and to remain aloof. Failure to enter into the spirit of the occasion indicates a lack of consideration.

Be punctual in your arrival, and do nothing that would upset the schedule of events. Dinner at 7:00 p.m. means arrival 15 minutes before that time, period. Later than that, the hosts will smile, and hate you for throwing the schedule off. If delays beyond your control happen, call and let them know when you expect to arrive. Really good friends show up at the cocktail hour right on time, not a half hour later. The first half hour is tough for the hosts, wondering when people will show up. So get there on time, show the flag, and your friends will rest easier. Remain as a guest no longer than originally invited, even if urged to do so. Prolong the visit only if the invitation to remain is so insistent there is no possible doubt of the desires of the host.

Guests pitch in. **Overnight guests** make their beds, wash dishes, keep the bathroom neat, take out the garbage, and stand ready to accept more complex chores. It's enough that your hosts are providing free food and shelter, so don't expect them to organize your every waking minute. After you arrive, suggest a few things you would like to do and see, and find out how those plans fit into the agenda your hosts have planned. A little planning and accommodation on both sides will minimize misunderstanding and disappointment.

A thoughtful guest knows when to disappear. However close you may be to the hosts, odds are you don't customarily spend 14 hours a day with them even when you lived together. If you don't take the initiative, they might feel obligated to entertain you all the time, and by the end of the first day, your friendship will be strained or history.

Upon departure, immediately write a letter of appreciation to the host, and, if appropriate, send a gift because of courtesies extended to you. Always acknowledge hospitality and courtesies extended to you. For the host, bring or send a gift such as a book, a classic video, flowers, a bottle of good wine, candy, or other expressions of appreciation to be enjoyed by all. Clothing, jewelry, and art are usually gifts to avoid. Gifts can be presented the minute you arrive, during your stay, or sent very soon after you leave. Sometimes it is good to gather ideas during your stay for the appropriate gift.

Remember that even mild social drinking will dull one's reflexes and sensibilities. Drink only in moderation, if at all. If case something breaks which you can replace, replace it at your earliest convenience. If it cannot be replaced, give a gift they will enjoy. State how sorry you are for the mishap immediately and again in your thank you letter.

Today's manners should inspire you to go up to a host who has just dropped a platter of food all over the floor in front of the guests and help clean up the mess. Then pat her arm and tell her to forget about it – "It doesn't matter at all."

D. Rising for Others

Except when seated at a dining table, rise and stand every time someone from the outside – a guest, a peer or an elder – enters the room. Men and women alike, or of any age, should rise and step forward to greet their callers, just as you would rise and step forward to greet a new guest at an event or at the office.

It is a time-honored tradition that gentlemen rise as a woman or elder enters the room. Remain standing until they are seated. Also, men rise when women rise if they are on a date, or seated next to you. The exception to this rule is if the woman is a frequent visitor to your place, and then would be treated as a member of the group.

The best rule is to stand, even if it is just your neighbor next door popping in to borrow something. Rise automatically and say something in greeting, even if it is as brief as, "Hello, Mrs. Smith." You don't need to keep popping up and down every time Mrs. Smith comes through the room on her visit. Once is enough.

Stand by your chair at the dining table (or in the restaurant) until all guests and women are seated. (See 2.B., page 9.)

Your posture is important, so stand tall! The person who stands erect looks best. A slouch or sprawl is unappealing, and clothes do not hang right. Men have less problem **sitting** than women because pants allow more latitude. Men look best sitting erect with both feet on the floor, or one leg crossed over the other above the knee. Women should sit with their knees together, crossing the feet at the ankles if they wish. In a deep easy chair, sit slightly sideways, knees together, or legs crossed, and skirts pulled down.

E. Removing Hat and Gloves

Hats, caps, and gloves are always removed when entering homes, classrooms, clubs, churches, private offices, and elsewhere when the surroundings suggest that is proper. While walking through the lobby of a public building, or in an elevator, it is not necessary to remove a hat or cap. <u>Never</u>, even when informal, should a baseball hat be worn during a meal (a common mistake today). A gentleman, when stopping to converse with a lady or elder on the street, removes his hat in respect and deference, and remains uncovered during the time until they say "goodbye." When visiting with another man on the street, a man can keep his hat on, lifting or touching the hat as a sign of greeting. A woman, however, may keep her hat on, except when working and during meals. (See page 56.)

F. Offering an Arm, Opening Doors

When appropriate, a man offers his right arm to assist a woman, such as walking on ice, on a slope, or on stairs. The woman stays next to the stair railing, "upstair" from the man, in case of a trip or fall. Anyone sure-footed and stable may offer an arm to an elder or a frail person when it appears that courtesy would be appreciated. Generally it is improper to offer an arm unless there is a real necessity of assistance, such as on ice and in deep snow. At formal dinners, a gentleman offers his right arm to his dinner partner in escorting her to the dining room. A group of friends should walk no more than two abreast to avoid distracting passersby.

Thanks to the feminist movement, there is more common sense when it comes to **door** handling. With the exception of the elderly, handicapped, and the pregnant – who always get preferential treatment – the holding of doors is an equal opportunity activity. Just be courteous and kind, and do what is handy for others. It is still good manners for men to let female companions go first into doors, elevators, revolving doors, and rooms.

Today's manners make you realize that it's not worthwhile wondering who should go into an elevator or through the revolving door first, but it is worthwhile rushing to help an elderly or disabled person through any door that could be inconvenient, difficult, or unsafe. Any courteous person – man or woman – holds open the door for the person following, unless that person is some distance behind. When an elevator stops, the person nearest the door gets out first.

Women should be **escorted** back to their homes, cars, or anywhere where their safety may be in question. Men should be sensitive to those concerns, and escort women accordingly. The custom requiring a man to walk on the outside when strolling with a woman to defend her against runaway horses, garbage, and mud is outdated, but is still proper. In large cities, the man may want to walk on the inside to protect her from muggers or purse snatchers who may lurk in the doorway. The old way looks right, feels right, and maybe the most danger is still from the street side. If in doubt, the gentleman offers his right arm.

G. The Gentlemen Helps Her...

Into a taxi, a gentleman opens the door, stands aside, and lets her in first. That is, unless, she is dressed such that she would have to slide over the hump in the floor, messing up her long dress and snagging her dress or her high heels. If you can go around to the other side, do so. If not, it may make more sense to say "It may be easier for me to go first." When wearing a skirt, a woman getting into the back seat of a taxi should put one foot in, slide in sideways, sit down, and pull the other foot in. To get out, put both feet out, edge forward, and stand up. A woman enters first, exists last.

On **public transportation** – like subways, trains, and buses – a man offers a helping hand for her to get on first, ready to catch her should she slip and fall. A man gets off first so he can turn around to offer her a hand on the step across or down. However it makes no sense for men to lag way behind letting every woman get on first. Keep the traffic moving is proper traffic etiquette. Men or women should give their seats to anyone who is disabled, elderly, pregnant, or carrying a child or bulky packages.

The man should check coats in the cloak room, for him and his companion. Helping women with their **coats** looks and feels right. Do hold the coat with both hands at her shoulder height (not yours). Rest your left hand on her left shoulder, and dip your right hand slightly allowing her to place her right arm into the armhole without raising her elbow too high. Help her look graceful by not having her elbows flapping like wings looking for the sleeve.

H. Splitting the Check

Women are more aware of the high cost of entertaining, and frequently pay their way. Romance no longer has to mean bankruptcy for gentlemen. In modern times, who asks whom first pays, and the next time the other pays. After that, if you still like each other, common sense dictates the one with the most resources and income pays accordingly. Simple equity and common sense should be your guide. A woman offers to pay before they arrive at a restaurant, and notifies the waiter that she would like the bill when ordering. Otherwise the waiter automatically brings it to the man. With a group, a couple agrees how to handle the check before they arrive.

If you are well-heeled, be generous and pick up the entire tab. But necessity will usually demand separate checks, or splitting checks, which may make everyone feel rotten. Penny pinchers are sure they paid for someone else's dessert, and generous spenders feel inhospitable. Even the waiter is convinced his tip is shortchanged. Everyone looks bad when the calculator comes out between the dessert dishes.

If you are part of a large group, there is no way around it. The best way however, is to split the check equally, plus tip, by the number of people paying. Next time, you may have a more expensive entree, and it will even out. If ever in doubt, the gentleman pays. If she has class (and a job), she'll pick it up next time, or return the favor with a nice gift.

I. Singing and Serenading

Serenading is a traditional fraternal activity, and a means of keeping excellent relations between your chapter and others on campus. Whether performed by the entire chapter or a small singing group, it is impressive when done well, using harmony, and most noticeable when the group is dressed well. While serenading, you are a guest, so be respectful of other's property. Do not stand on chairs to get a better view, etc.

Another wonderful custom is singing at the table. This is not done to prolong the meal, but occurs at the beginning of the meal or between the main course and dessert as the tables are being cleared. Mealtime is an excellent opportunity for singing, as the atmosphere is relaxed and provides for a time of fellowship. Besides, this is when you can get the most voices together. This also provides an opportunity to practice for serenades, interfraternal singing competition, and other occasions when polished renditions are desired. Singing helps promote fellowship, and gives an upbeat lift of morale to the group.

J. Flowers, Notes, and Other Appreciation

Manners help you notice candy, roses, or a gift in a shop window. So you buy a small item to bring home to a person you care about, or who needs a day brightener. A friend gives an unexpected gift with a card that reads: "With love, from Angie, just because it feels like spring outside today, and I wanted you to have some of the first daffodils to brighten up your day!"

When invited to a social event, write the host a thank-you note within twenty-four hours – even if your traveling companion is also invited and writes a note, you should write one too. If you were the guest of honor, you would send flowers or a present (with a note) to the host the next day.

The holidays provide the perfect opportunity to renew the acquaintances you made during college or travels. Send each person a newsy Christmas or New Year's card, in which you mention how much you enjoyed seeing him. Give your address and phone number, and say how much you hope he will visit.

Thank you letters are a must in polite society and they should be short and informal. Send one every time you are given a present, sent flowers, asked to lunch or dinner, asked to a concert, the opera, the theater, even a movie. Write a thank-you note whenever you are the recipient of a favor – such as when a person writes a letter of reference to help you get a job, or finds you an apartment, or serves as a matchmaker for you, or provides information to help you out.

A thank-you letter can be as short as three sentences:

> *Dear Larry,*
>   *Lunch today was splendid – in every respect – the restaurant, the food, the company, and the conversation! Many thanks. It was nice catching up.*
>
>   *Sincerely,*

When some people receive a present, they write a trite, blah, nothing note, such as:

> *Dear Marie,*
>   *Thank you for your nice gift. It was very sweet of you, and I appreciate it.*

After reading a note like that, Marie probably doesn't even remember why she gave a gift! Others thankfully enthuse a little and tell the donor how they are using the present:

> *Dear Marie,*
>   *You cannot imagine what pleasure your scarf has given me. The pinks and blues of the paisley print are lovely; they pick up my tired winter dresses and make them look fresh again. I receive compliments on the scarf every time I wear it, and I seem to be wearing it constantly. If you had spent weeks trying to find the perfect gift for me, you could not have chosen better. (Perhaps you did spend weeks finding it!) Bless you. I really am delighted with your choice.*
>   *Sincerely yours,*

Some people think that thank-you notes are for women only. Perhaps it seems that only brides write thank-you notes for wedding presents, and you can recall that Mom wrote for Dad to Aunt Sally for the Christmas gift, but <u>all</u> people of class write thank-you notes. When someone does something nice for you, say "thank you." Period. And besides, even nineties women are impressed with a note saying "thanks for the terrific evening." The biggest trick about saying thank you is doing it. Postage costs very little.

K. Apologies

Apologize when you've irked anyone, even if you feel innocent. Always take the first step to ask forgiveness, and keep those lines of communication open. Friends and family may become greatly upset with each other for the most insignificant reasons. Deal with any negative at once, so that a small sore does not become a festering wound.

Letters of apology are to be done immediately any time you have hurt someone's feelings. Inadvertently, or purposely, a tart tongue, a clever and witty put-down, critical remarks about others while they, unbeknownst to you, are standing listening to your group, all demand action. Whether you make an unkind remark about someone's new outfit and it gets back to him or you take a crack at someone's ideas in front of your colleagues, you should apologize – verbally, right on the spot, and then in writing, with a personal note hand-delivered within twenty-four hours of the incident.

Apologies never totally make up for something, but at least they are better than nothing. When, for example, the person who has wronged you takes no action, your resentment can fester over time and eat away at you, ruining your productivity. Therefore, knowing how you demand some kind of retribution for a wrong done you, remember everyone else's need, too, even when you are at fault. It helps to send flowers (from a man or a woman, to a man or a woman) with your note of apology. There's something serene and soothing about flowers. Your note can be long and detailed, if you are trying to justify how this unpleasant experience happened, or it can be as short as this:

> *Dear Lee,*
> *It shouldn't have happened, but it did. There is no excuse for what I said. I just hope that since I acted inappropriately, you will show your usual big heart and forgive me. There's a lot to forgive, but I want you to know I am truly, truly sorry. If you forgive me, I shall be forever in your debt. Please put me in your debt!*
> *Sincerely yours,*

5. SELF-PROTECTION FROM SOCIAL ABUSE

A. Courtesy and Dignity

Show respect for others at all times. A respect for deference means no back talk, acting fresh, or defying authority. Respect for elders, parents, grandparents, teachers, clergy, police, and anyone else in a position of authority should be instinctive. Rules of deference have developed over the centuries to enhance living in harmony, by respecting experience and level of responsibility. Manners are based on good character, which translates to kindness, compassion, thoughtfulness – and yes, love.

Courteous people allow everyone to have his dignity, from a person of title and rank, to one who has lost everything, even hope. This means we are not critical or judgmental of others, but are kind. The misfortune of others is not our blessing. We should be tolerant of those who are different. We should be discreet in public, not drawing undue attention to ourselves with actions, loud voice, or boorish behavior. We defer to those of age, rank, title, or position, using the proper form of address. These are the qualities we want in a leader, and we trust and respect these virtues in others. We want to surround ourselves with people of quality, and we should set the example.

Never miss an opportunity to make others feel better about the world. When your neighbor casually mentions that it's his 25th wedding anniversary, so you give him the bottle of wine you were saving in the fridge for your own special occasion.

B. Social Drinking

Business entertaining and hosting often involve situations where alcoholic beverages are present. The period of time between the arrival of guests, and the beginning of the meal, was named logically the "cocktail hour." Lounges often feature a "happy hour" after work during which time colleagues can unwind from their work day before heading home. Cocktail parties (no dinner) are very much a part of the social scene. How you handle alcohol will influence how people feel about you as a colleague, friend, spouse, or potential employee.

As with table etiquette, there are customs and protocols that should be observed in any professional or social setting. Discussed here are customs from the business world. Socializing may help advance your career as you get to know the boss, entertain key clients, and meet dignitaries. But over-imbibing is career suicide.

Watch the booze. The days of the three martini liquid lunch are gone. Avoid excessive use of alcohol at all times, as it can lead to indiscretions, coarse language, and international incidents. "Drunk and stupid" is a redundant phrase.

One drink before dinner is enough. A glass or two of wine during a meal is okay, and an after-dinner drink can wrap up your conversation for the evening very nicely. If you are still thirsty, drink pop, mineral water, soda, juice, coffee, or other beverages. Have no more than three drinks at a reception or cocktail party. To have more is to court trouble, and draw unfavorable attention your way.

If you do not wish to drink, don't. If you wish to minimize questions, hold a glass of tonic water with a slice of lemon or lime, or a glass of ginger ale. They resemble a mixed drink, and quench your thirst. When offered a drink, the most diplomatic way of getting out of ordering alcohol is to smile and say "no thank you" without further explanation. If they persist, cite a personal reason such as, "No thank you, I'm driving," or "I'm on a diet," or "I'm on medication that is not compatible with alcohol," etc. When pressed, and as a last resort, it is okay to say, "No thank you, I choose not to drink." Be careful of your tone when you say that as it may set a social barrier which implies that the other person is a lush. The other person should be made to feel comfortable to take a drink if they wish. When a toast is offered, it is fine to use a glass of any beverage, or go through the motion of lifting the glass to your lips.

Choosing a wine. Entire books are written about this subject, and people make careers out of the study of wine. Here, the basics will be presented, and further study is up to you.

It is a sign of savoir-faire (French for "knowing tact in any situation") to be able to choose an appropriate beverage. At a fine restaurant, it is gauche to drink hard liquor before dinner as it numbs the taste buds for the meal. Similarly, sweet wine before meals diminishes the appetite. A dry wine or sherry is appropriate.

The wine for the meal is selected <u>after</u> the meal has been chosen. The host should ask the guests for preferences before making the selection. If you are not familiar with the wine list, ask the wine steward to recommend a red or white wine as you peruse the list. Usually they are listed in order of price, so you can point to an approximate price range to let the steward subtly know what you are willing to pay. Indicate your preference for domestic or imported wine, red, white, or rosé. If on a tight budget, order the "house wine."

The traditional rule is that white wine is served with white meat, red wine with red meat. White meats include turkey, chicken, fish, seafood, pork, and veal. Red meats include beef, game, and duck. However, feel free to order any wine that you and your guests will enjoy.

When the wine is expensive, the steward will bring you the cork. The cork should be moist, and the color and texture indicate whether the wine has been stored correctly. Sniff the wine without touching the glass to be sure the wine is not spoiled, and usually the steward can detect that upon opening the bottle. However, unless a connoisseur, avoid making comments, just indicate that it is fine, unless you smell vinegar. You will be asked to taste the wine. Bring the glass up to your nose to smell the "bouquet" (not acidic), take a small taste, and slightly swirl the wine in your mouth for a short time. The only time you send a bottle of wine back is if it is spoiled. Red wines over ten years old are opened early to allow them to "breathe" before they are served. White wines do not need to "breathe."

Red wines are served at room temperature, and the bowl of the glass can be held delicately in your fingers, since the heat from your fingers will not adversely affect the flavor of the wine. Do not grasp the glass with your entire hand, nor use both hands to lift the glass to your lips. When drinking chilled white wines, your fingers should not touch the bowl of the glass, as heat from your fingers may affect the flavor. Hold the stem of the glass gently between your fingers.

After-dinner Drinks. Hard liquor is served usually as an after dinner drink or "digestif" (dee-jes-TEEF) – a French word suggesting it will aid the digestive process. Entire books and dictionaries are written about this, too, and there are many different kinds of mixed drinks and liqueurs from around the world. It is strictly a matter of taste and preference. However, in the business world, it is best to keep it simple with the basics, such as brandy, scotch, vodka, gin, wine, and beer. Ordering a "Screaming Orgasm," a "Coalminer's Breakfast," or a "Fuzzy Navel" will not win you any points for elegance.

Handling Drunks. When colleagues and friends get drunk, rowdy, or demonstrate any socially inappropriate behavior, they should be protected from hurting themselves or others, professionally, socially, or physically. Escort drunks home or call a taxi; do not let them drive. Escort them away from a crowd of people so they lose their "audience," and do not offend or abuse anyone. Be calm. Speak quietly and gently take control of the situation. Drunks are difficult to handle, and it may take two or three friends to bring a difficult situation under control. They will thank you the next day after the influence of alcohol has worn off. **Inappropriate behavior cannot be tolerated – drunk or not.**

C. Date Rape

If you feel uneasy about going through with an evening as planned, or being alone with a date, do not go through with it. Invite another couple to join you, have a sudden change of plans, or be around other people. The feelings or intuition may have a good basis, and it pays to be careful. You may not have seen your date under the influence before, or he may be coming on too fast. Most women (84%) are raped by a person they know, most are between the ages of 16 and 24, and 57% of rapes occur on a date.

Women should not put themselves into vulnerable situations with men they do not know well, either personally or by reputation. One should go only to public events until you do get to know him. Women should not leave friends at a party or at an apartment if they are drunk and not in control. Men need to stop condoning potentially dangerous, aggressive behavior of friends. Sex must be based on mutual consent. If a person is not capable of giving consent due to intoxication, drugs, or unconsciousness, then any sex is legally defined as rape.

Date rape is a serious crime, best avoided by thinking, talking, listening, and less alcohol rather than more. It is never okay for a man to force himself on a woman. "No" means "no," and a date has the right to stop sexual activity at any point. Respect that, as some individuals are not certain what they want from a sexual situation until it unfolds. Games may be played by women saying "no" (as "good girls" are expected to say) while meaning "yes," and some women say "yes" when drunk, often regretting it the next day. **Men and women are responsible for their actions at all times, drunk or not, even if the desires are out of control.**

Do not let desires control your actions, and be mindful that the other person may want intimacy and affection, but not intercourse. There are sexual activities (safe sex) you may both <u>agree</u> to other than intercourse. **Pause, ask, and clarify** if you have any doubt what your partner is thinking, feeling and agreeing to. Communicate your limits clearly. Don't be afraid to say "no." Turning someone down for sex is not a rejection of you as a person. It is expressing an opinion about a single act at that time. Sex involves a complex array of feelings and emotion, as well as the one dimension most talked about, physical pleasure. Good manners include talking to your partner about sex, mutually agreeing, and being sensitive to each other.

D. Sex and Condoms

For those who do not abstain, precautions must be taken. Because of sexually transmitted diseases, especially AIDS and herpes, sex is no longer a taboo subject to talk about. No longer do you have to hem and haw about saying yes or no about having sex with someone. No is okay, and if you want to say yes, it is on your terms – safe sex only! And use birth control to avoid pregnancy. At least use a condom. No pleasure or moment of passion is worth putting your life and health at risk. Men and women can no longer be shy or embarrassed about talking about, and insisting on, protection. Many people are carriers of sexually transmitted diseases, and don't know it. A 1991 *New England Journal of Medicine* article reported that only seven percent (one in fourteen!) of people with the HIV virus told their sexual partners they had the virus. Don't trust or assume they are not carriers. Assume if they have had sex in the last five years, they may be.

If you are sexually active, use birth control <u>and</u> keep a condom supply handy in advance (men and women). If not prepared, just announce "Since we are not prepared, we'll just have to wait until we are. Let's skip tonight." Men and women need to teach each other to be responsible. Note that condoms have a fairly high rate of failure when used to prevent pregnancy. Condoms can, and do, break or slip off. Wear before genital contact starts.

E. Sexual Harassment

Sexual harassment is <u>unwanted</u>, <u>repeated</u> sexual attention, by either gender. It is the inappropriate sexualization of an otherwise nonsexual relationship. It falls into categories, differing on severity. They are:

- Gender harassment - sexist remarks and behavior
- Seductive behavior - inappropriate staring, leering, or flirting
- Sexual bribery - promise of rewards for sexual activity, compromising invitations
- Sexual coercion - demanded or forced sexual activity by threat of punishment
- Sexual assault - gross sexual imposition like touching, fondling, patting, grabbing, or physical assault

At least half, and as many as 80% of all women experience sexual harassment at some point during their academic and working life. It is a wide-spread problem experienced by a majority of women. It is illegal if a job or promotion depends on submission to demands, or the harassment creates a hostile environment, even if job security or promotion is not affected.

Sexual harassment is about power, not sex, i.e. the powerful taking license to exploit the less powerful. Women are sexually harassed more than men, but men are also too often the victims of sexual harassment. There is no such thing as mutual consent in a sexual relationship between a professor and student, or a supervisor and an employee. The less powerful have no position from which to negotiate so they are vulnerable, and the power rests with just one person. Livelihoods, approval, psychological well-being, and self esteem are tied up in pleasing the person with power. Work and academic environments need to be desexualized, i.e. become places of greater professionalism.

Deal with sexual harassment; do not ignore it. Inform the harasser that the extra attention is unwanted. Make clear you find the behavior offensive. Refuse all invitations firmly.

If harassment persists, write a memo to the harasser requesting it stop (keep a copy). Write down details of each incident including comments, your response, date, time, and place. Try to find witnesses and other victims. Two accusations are much harder to ignore. You may want to consider using grievance procedures or channels detailed in your workplace or university in severe cases.

The first thing to say to victims of sexual harassment is, "I'm sorry this has happened. You didn't do anything wrong." The victim is not to blame. Of course, never should someone be accused of sexual harassment unless it is true. Accusing the innocent is a high-stakes power play where everyone will likely lose.

6. PUBLIC CONDUCT

A. Campus

Students are on campus not just to absorb knowledge, but also to learn how to apply this new information as you prepare for your profession. A liberal arts education is meant to prepare students to be worldly citizens, to take their place in society responsibly, and contribute to the community in which they live. Much of higher education occurs out of the classroom, and you have a responsibility to round out your education with these experiences.

As a campus citizen, you have some responsibilities. Not everyone will be a leader on campus, although many do develop valuable leadership skills at this time. Everyone does have a chance to influence issues, other people, and the course of many events. Your responsibilities include:

- **Keep informed**. Group decisions can only be effective when students make an effort to be informed. Listen with an open mind to all sides of an issue, giving others a chance to express their viewpoints. You make better decisions when you are informed. Vote intelligently.

- **Participate**. Woody Allen suggested that "80% of success is just showing up." Get involved and contribute your time and talents to class efforts, professional groups, and worthy organizations. Then attend meetings with regularity and punctuality. Understand parliamentary procedure to best exercise your rights and duties of membership. Seek opportunity, not security. A boat in a harbor is safe, but in time the bottom rots out.

- **Leadership**. The world is in great need of leadership if we are to solve the economic, political, educational, environmental, social problems that lie before us. Fraternities and sororities are great leadership training grounds, as indicated by the number of Greeks who are leaders. Nationally, Greeks are less than 2% of the population, but provide over 80% of the leadership in business, government, and education. Of the people listed in "Who's Who," three-fourths are Greek. The Greek experience teaches you how to work with others, provides opportunities to test your leadership skills in a win-win environment, stresses that you be sensitive to others and the importance of good performance over intentions. That is how 2% equals 80%. College is time and opportunity to test and hone your leadership and team skills in a safe environment among friends; a place to gain confidence as you gain competence. Remember the lead sled dog has the best view.

- **Be responsible**. Assist leaders in their tasks. Meet your financial obligations promptly, make reports promptly, strive for excellence and integrity, offer emotional support, openly communicate, be positive. Challenge members to abide by their obligations, and confront those who violate them. Success or failure depends not only on the leaders, but on all people on campus.

- **Integrity**. Sandbox politics is all too common on campus, in government, and in business. Sometimes friends give undue favor to friends, appoint unqualified persons to key positions, vote for those we know rather than the most qualified, and use positions of power inappropriately. If seems if you can give a reason to justify it, it is okay, or it is excused because someone else did it too. Wrong.

  Loyalty to your friends can be a great virtue, but not at the expense of honesty, truth, fairness, and your integrity. Your victories need to come from real accomplishment, not favor. You need to conduct your affairs in such a way to be proud. Stop doing what does not make you proud, less you shame yourself and those with whom you affiliate.

Evil triumphs when good people do nothing. Confront and challenge those who play sandbox politics. Insist on fairness, honesty, integrity, and other values that make a civil society. You cannot have pride, self-esteem, or confidence without it.

We learn, labor, live, love, and leisure in groups. From the simple family unit to a complex organization, from classes to sports teams, we experience groups every day. Our affiliation with groups gives us a sense of identity, and where we are going. Our résumés not only report our accomplishments and abilities, but also the groups we are a part of from our college days to memberships in various organizations. Although each of us is an individual with distinct characteristics, we also have an identity based on formal and informal groups.

Group identity can make a positive statement as, "Our college is innovative and fully accredited," "Our fraternity stresses scholarship," or "Our company is committed to customer service." It can also be negative: "My community is dying," "Our company has a high turnover of people," "My friends all do drugs," or "Our fraternity hazes our pledges." Our groups help us identify who we are, what we are about, and where we are going. They help us measure change in ourselves and others.

It is important to affiliate with groups that create positive influences in our lives, and to help make the groups we join as positive as they can be. It should be a goal to leave groups better than we found them. Just as we benefitted from those who came before us, we need to provide for those who will follow.

B. Volunteering

Volunteer service is the rent we pay for the privileges we enjoy. Fraternity and sorority members have a great sense of community spirit, and sense of responsibility for others. No other college group raises so much money, or gives more time to charitable, social, political, educational, and cultural causes. **Social responsibility** is very much a part of professional character too, getting involved in the community. Do get involved, giving of your time, expertise, and money to enhance the quality of life. This is a way to say "thank you" for our blessings in life, and to pay for our rent on earth as long as we are here. Not only should we aid society through service, but we must advance society through our contributions.

You can contribute to your community and your campus by giving of your time, talent (skills), and treasure (funds). If you are going to contribute, give smartly, meaning give to causes you really believe in, and do not spread yourself too thin. Make an impact. Professionals usually give five percent (**5%**) of their income, and five percent of their time to philanthropy, per year. Remember that you are directly paying a small portion of your education costs, as alumni and taxpayers are picking up the rest of the tab because they believe in the value of education. As you have received, so should you prepare for those who follow.

C. Community

Etiquette – the art of making others feel comfortable, important and at ease – is an important consideration whether you are about your community or traveling. Having superior manners and etiquette will set you apart from others, raising your head above the crowd. It will make you feel good, and draw favorable attention to you as you enter the professional world.

Courtesies to observe with those you encounter during your day. Manners with the **professionals** who serve you:

- Respect all professionals, whether it is your lawyer, doctor, or banker for that person's education and experience.

- When professionals perform a service exceptionally well, let them know it.

- Keep your appointments, and be punctual.

- Don't take for granted anyone you consider a personal friend, and most certainly do not try to get free advice in social situations.

Your manners with **waiters**:

- Give them your attention when they come to tell you the specialties and take your order. Don't expect that to be done properly if everyone is joking, talking, and paying no attention.

- If you keep changing your mind, don't lose your temper over subsequent errors. (It's not the waiter's fault.)

- Call quietly to the "Waiter" or "Waitress" to get their attention; don't snap your fingers, whistle, or shout.

- When something goes wrong with the order, do not voice criticisms at the waiter that everyone can hear. There are other factors – kitchen help, for example – that could be responsible for what went wrong. When something is incorrect, inform the waiter in a quiet voice that cannot be heard by others.

- When things go well, praise him and thank him – and tell the owner or manager, "Your waiter did a great job for us tonight."

D. With Elders

Show respect for elders at all times. Deference and respect for experience and age is a time-honored tradition for good reasons. They have extensive experience, accumulated wisdom, and have lived through the cycles of life. Respect for parents, grandparents, teachers, clergy, police, and anyone else in a position of authority, should be instinctive.

Untraditionally, some parents insist that their children call all their friends by their first names. It may be very difficult for a child to call his parents' friends by their first names and all other adults (such as teachers, the doctor, the minister, and the dance instructor) by their title and last names. Some parents go to the extent of having their young children call them by their first names – all in the desire to show independence, perhaps hoping to be perceived as nonconformists. It is a free country. Parents can teach their children whatever they wish, but by encouraging nonconformist usage, it is just that much more difficult for their children to learn deference and respect for older people.

Show deference to people who are senior, rather than treating them with the same "first-name, slap-on-the-back, we're-all-equal" attitude. Many a senior executive in his sixties winces upon meeting a young executive from another company who immediately calls him by his first name.

E. Public Image

A simple definition of a really admired person – someone who has real class – is a person who has only one kind of manners: the caring kind. The late Ambassador Clare Boothe Luce (a role model and mentor to many) answered a reporter who had asked for a definition of a "really classy person." The reporter's notebook and pen were poised for a typically long Luce dissertation. "A person with class is someone you want to be around – all the time," she answered simply. The reporter paused, and finally asked, "That's it?" "There's no need for anything more," she replied.

As individuals, we often spend so much time philosophizing about the big picture that we lose sight of the small details. It is the small detail that is capable of making another person lose respect for us or, conversely, look upon us as a hero. In public it is important to remember that it is rude to disrupt other lives, whether it be at a movie, on public transportation, at the beach, in a mall, or at the airport. Do not make a lot of noise; i.e. be pleasant and avoid upsetting others.

Dress comfortably, but nicely. Many well-heeled Americans dress sloppily when they fly today. A person clad in a beat-up t-shirt, sawed off jeans, and monk's sandals hardly makes a great impression when he or she steps off a plane in another country. The well-dressed, neat young American, on the other hand, makes an instant, favorable impression on people from other countries. "Don't disgrace your country!" mothers used to call after their sons when they left for faraway lands, and by that they meant, "Stay well groomed while you travel, whatever you do!"

It also helps your image (and makes everyone who has to look at you feel much better, too) if you carry your personal effects in suitcases, rather than in a series of plastic bags that look as if they just came from the supermarket. Some of the most affluent seem to be careless about this.

F. Flag Customs

Laws have been written to govern the use of the flag to ensure a proper respect for the Stars and Stripes. Customs dictate observances in regard to its use. The flag should be displayed on national and state holidays and other days as proclaimed by the President of the United States. On Memorial Days, the flag should be flown at half-mast until noon.

Flags are not flown at night or in inclement weather. The flag may be displayed outdoors 24 hours a day if properly lighted during the hours of darkness. Otherwise, only from sunrise to sunset. Public buildings should display the flag daily on or near the building. Always hoist the flag briskly, lower it ceremoniously. When flown half-mast for mourning, the flag should be hoisted to the peak for a moment, and then lowered to half-mast. When retired, it should be raised to the peak before lowered for the day.

The United States flag is always accorded the place of honor on a platform, positioned on its own right, i.e. to the speaker's right (audience's left). Other flags should be positioned to the left of the speaker.

When displaying the flag against the wall, vertically or horizontally, it should be placed behind and above the speaker. The flag's union (stars) should be at the top, to the flag's own right and the observer's left.

When displayed with flags of states and organizations, the U.S. flag should be at the center and at the highest point of the group. When displayed with flags from other nations, the staffs are of equal height, with the U.S. flag in the position of honor at the flag's right, which is the extreme left as the flags are viewed. International usage forbids the display of the flag of one nation above that of another nation in time of peace. No flag may fly above or to the right of the U.S. flag.

Presentation of Colors. The flag should be saluted when raised or lowered as part of a ceremony, or when it passes by in a parade or in review. All persons, except those in military uniform, should face the flag and stand at attention with the right hand over the heart. A man should remove his hat with his right hand, holding the hat at his left shoulder. Those in uniform should give the military salute. Foreign visitors should stand at attention, but need not salute.

National Anthem. When the *Star Spangled Banner* is played, everyone should remain standing at attention, face the flag (or the music if there is no flag), and most properly of all, with the right hand over the heart. Military personnel stand and salute. Men remove their hats.

When the flag is used to cover a casket, it should be so placed that the union is at the head and over the left shoulder. The flag should not touch the ground, or be lowered into the grave.

At all times, respect should be shown our flag. The U.S. flag should never touch anything beneath it – ground, water, or merchandise. Protect it from being soiled, torn, or damaged in any way. Never use the flag to cover a table or drape a podium or platform. Decorate using red, white, and blue bunting, placing the blue strip on top, red on the bottom. Always allow the flag to fall free, never drawn back, nor up or festooned.

Flags should not be used as a piece of clothing, a drape, bedding, or as any part of a costume or athletic uniform. Nothing should be placed on a flag such as letters, words, figures, designs, pictures, or drawings. A flag patch can be affixed to uniforms of military, firemen, police, or members of patriotic organizations.

When the flag is in poor condition, no longer a fitting emblem for display, it should be destroyed in a dignified way, preferably by burning in private.

7. CORRESPONDENCE

A. Personal Letters

The telephone has almost completely replaced letters for communicating in the last decade. Letter writing is becoming a lost art. However, all of us get excited when receiving a letter from a friend or family member with news and expressions of caring. There are certain times when the telephone is not adequate such as expressing some compliments and when exact wording adds to the thoughtfulness. When least expected, letters have the most impact. The letters we like most, are those that carry the writer's personality with them, and it seems as if they are sitting beside you.

To write good letters, pick a time when you're relaxed and feeling up. Use a comfortable desk, chair, and a good light by which to write. Use an excellent pen with the right point for you. Use black or a dark color ink. Use good stationery – good quality stock, and in an appropriate color: Gray, cream, or white for office stationery; ditto for men's personal stationery. Use any pastel, gray, cream or white for women's personal stationery.

Either write by hand or type a neat letter. Think before you write. Make an outline of the points you wish to cover, and you will write cohesively – without forgetting any point. Always, edit your letter for spelling, grammar, and content. Read it carefully and make corrections (the wonders of a computer!). Letters can be brief, if the message is well delivered. Stress the positive and never start or finish a letter with anything negative.

Research the address of your recipient, including the proper title, postal code, and any other necessary particulars, especially for business letters. If you are writing to people you don't know, and may not even know their gender, call their chapter house or business to find out: "Excuse me, I'm calling to find out if I should address a letter to M<u>r</u>. Chris Clark or M<u>s</u>. Chris Clark." For the past thirty years, parents have been more creative in naming their children. Don't assume you know. If you guess wrong, you have made a poor impression, and that may imply you don't care. Do your research!

When writing to people with professional titles, do not use "Mr.," "Ms.," or "Dr." when using their degree after the surname. For example write: John Smith, M.D. (not Dr. John Smith, M.D.), Mary Smith, R.N. (not Ms. Mary Smith, R.N.), Robert Smith, Ph.D. (not Dr. Robert Smith, Ph.D.). When you see initials on the letterhead after someone's name, use those initials after his surname when you write.

Using "Ms." is no longer controversial, and it is here to stay. "Miss" is only used with young women up to eighteen, and when you know that is their choice. People over 50 may prefer the old tradition of "Miss" and "Mrs." A woman's marital status has no bearing on her title, so Ms. equals Mr. Use "Ms." on all correspondence, unless you know they prefer "Mrs." or "Miss," or when addressing a letter to "Mr. and Mrs. J. D. Smith."

Write from the "you" instead of the "I" perspective. Rather than writing "I am happy that you received the gift from us," write instead, "Thank you for your thoughtful note about the gift." Your reader will appreciate your perspective.

There are **letters better left unsent.** Do not write letters filled with **negatives**, misfortune, gloominess, and unhappiness. They serve no useful purpose, and can only worry, irritate, or depress the recipient. **Love letters** should be written so that you wouldn't mind your grandchildren reading them. Expect them to be saved. **Angry letters** filled with bitterness, fury, and rage are better left in the drawer after writing them. Letters written with strong emotions of any kind should be held for twenty-four hours and reread before being sent, or not sent at all.

Addressing Envelopes

To a married couple:	Mr. and Mrs. John Smith
To a married couple if she kept her family surname.	Mr. John Smith and Ms. Mary Olson *(note <u>and</u>)*
To a couple living together, but not married.	Mr. John Anderson Ms. Mary Parker *(note there is no <u>and</u>)*

Unmarried persons living together receive one invitation. They are listed on separate lines in alphabetical order, and there is no "and" joining their names. The "and" is reserved for married couples. The person with highest rank is always listed first (military rank, elected official, etc.)

With young men under the age of nine: Master William Smith
(after age nine, no title until high
school graduation, then "Mr.")

With young women under   Miss Mary Swanson
the age of eighteen:

See 1.E. for information regarding addressing people properly, page 4.

Negatives to watch for. Don't write letters when you're tired and disgruntled. Your physical state influences the way you write and the message you convey. Don't use a leaking pen or one running out of ink. Don't use an odd color; it makes your letter look eccentric. Don't dash off a note on a piece of legal paper or a sheet torn from a loose-leaf notebook. The quality of your communication takes on the quality of the paper upon which it is written. Never send a messy, crossed-out, ink-stained letter to anyone, even to someone who "won't mind." A long or rambling discourse – without a beginning, main part of text, or a conclusion – leaves the recipient feeling confused, unsure of your message, and wondering why you didn't care enough to do a good job. Never send letters with misspellings, grammatical, or punctuation errors. Never send a letter through the mail that you have not signed. Never send a letter without the date.

Closing a letter with a personal, warm message is best, but even a trite phrase, such as the following, is better than nothing:

> *"Hope our paths cross soon again."*
> *"I hope life is treating you well."*
> *"Here's wishing you lots of luck in your new venture."*
> *"Hope things are looking up (or going well) for you."*
> *"I hope to see you very soon."*

B. Invitations and RSVPs

When you are invited to something and asked to respond, protocol dictates that you do so promptly. Acceptance comes easy, so accept immediately. Two to three weeks advance is usual for most events, and a response should be within a week. Wedding invitations are sent six weeks or more in advance, and a reply within two weeks is fine. Oral invitations should be responded to immediately, unless you need to check your calendar or with your date. Unless asked to bring a date, do not bring one. If you cannot respond immediately because of tentative plans, give the host a time when you will reply, in plenty of time for them to make other arrangements or invite others if space is limited. DO NOT MAKE YOUR HOST CALL YOU BACK! The words "regrets only" on an invitation require a response only if you cannot attend. Be sure to call if you cannot attend, and if you don't call, attend.

Turning down an invitation is more difficult, especially if you don't want to go. A simple phrase will do: "Thank you for the invitation, but I'm afraid I can't make it. I have other plans, though I really appreciate you asking me." No further explanation is necessary. If the host rudely presses, be vague. Say you have work or family commitments.

Reciprocate. You should be on the giving, not always on the receiving, end. This means that you repay your friends' hospitality and kindnesses. Sometimes repayment takes a different form, but it's a repayment nevertheless. For example, if friends work hard to get you a part-time job, or a sought-after interview, you do not count the number of times they were guests without a return invitation.

Spontaneous invitations bond good friendships. Be sensitive to a friend's emotions. When you sense that a friend feels down, be ready to help. Perhaps what she needs is just an invitation to dinner and a pep talk; perhaps what he needs is just a sympathetic ear; perhaps what they need is the name of a good counselor.

Meet people when you're new to a job or locality. Take people to lunch! Invite your peers, even those higher up the corporate ladder, to a nice (not luxurious, just nice) restaurant for lunch. It's an investment. However, don't talk around the office about any of your lunch appointments, or people will think you're apple-polishing. These lunches will help you learn office procedures and politics – and allow you to show how personable, intelligent, and attractive you are in a relaxed situation. They allow you and the other person to get to know each other. You spend so many hours at work that it really is important to have friends there. They are a necessary support system in helping you get through the day. However, don't come on too strong with these invitations. Don't look overeager and aggressive. Be subtle and discreet.

C. Acceptance and Regrets

Answer all invitations as soon as possible (a.s.a.p.), at least within a week's time, and attend the event if you accepted the invitation. The well-mannered professional respects an RSVP on an invitation and is never an unexplained no-show. When a professional is a no-show at a corporate or social affair, it reflects badly on him or her and the company. RSVP stands for "repondez s'il vous plaît." That is French and a nice, old-fashioned, way of saying, "please respond." So please do.

D. Saying "Thank You"

Write thank-you notes within a week of receiving any gifts, favors, after each time you are a guest, and for any special courtesies extended to you. President and Mrs. Bush make time to write thank you notes, lots of them, and so should you. People who write thank you notes are remembered fondly, and get ahead in life because people say things about those courteous enough to note someone else's good efforts.

On a date, both should remember to thank the other person at the end of the date, even to write a thank-you note or send flowers within a week of the date – or the date's parents if a meal or a weekend visit at their home was involved. See 4.J., page 29, for further acts of appreciation.

8. PROFESSIONAL ETIQUETTE

A. Interviews

Preparing for the interview is a must. Learn all you can about the company where you are seeking employment. Use the library, secure a copy of the annual report if it is a publicly traded stock company, and read business publications such as *Fortune*, *Business Week*, *Forbes*, and the *Wall Street Journal*. Trade publications will have good information on the industry and the company. Visit with alumni and friends who already work for that company or one similar.

Before going to the interview, give serious thought about your professional goals and how this job opportunity might lead you toward your goals. How has previous experience qualified you for the position? What qualifications will they be looking for that you have? Be prepared to answer questions on your work history. Why did you leave? What did you accomplish? How did you grow? What are your strengths and weaknesses? Why do you think you are the best person for the job?

When you arrive, announce yourself and present your business card if you have one. Know the name of the interviewer, and pronounce it properly. If you are unsure, ask the secretary ahead of time. Ask the secretary whether he or she prefers Dr., Mr., Ms., Miss, or Mrs.

To help you be more productive in the interview:

- Be punctual. Never keep an interviewer waiting.

- Do not sit until invited to do so. Then sit in the chair indicated, or if none is, the chair across from the interviewer. Do not slouch, keep good posture and avoid nervous fidgeting.

- Dress conservatively. Dark suits are appropriate for men and women. The look is professional, not glamorous.

- Be neat. Shoes polished, hair cut and combed, no hems or cuffs frayed or raveling. Avoid excessive makeup, perfume, and jewelry.

- Do not smoke.

- Go alone, even if others you know are interviewing as well. Stand out alone.

- Speak with self-confidence. Answer the questions fully so that you amplify the facts on your résumé. Let the interviewer lead you into subjects with questions; do not waste his time on information he did not ask for. It is okay to ask questions about the job and company, but remember that "What are opportunities for career growth?" will impress him more than "How much vacation time do I get?" Indicate if you are definitely interested in the job – close the sale!

- Know when to leave. Some interviewers rise to indicate the termination of the interview, others terminate with a verbal phrase like "Thank you for coming." Be sensitive to this and rise promptly to leave.

- Be courteous. Throughout the interview follow the rules. Shake hands when you leave. Thank the interviewer for his time and interest. Smile. Keep good eye contact. Ask for a business card to ensure correct spelling of name, title, and address. Thank the secretary on the way out.

- It is common practice for potential employers to invite prospective employees out to dinner to observe the applicant's social skills, to watch you while eating, and to carry on an informal conversation. If interviewed over a meal, you will be thankful you practiced on formal meals at the chapter house. Be natural, courteous, and graceful, and don't order anything you can't eat gracefully. Drink no more than two cocktails – one would be even safer.

- After the interview, write a professional thank you letter. Not only is this good manners, but keeps your name before him for this job or maybe the next. If you have not heard from the company in two weeks, write or phone the interviewer, expressing continued interest in the position. If you still receive no reply, let it rest. Look elsewhere, and don't irritate them.

- Carry a good-quality pen in case you need to fill out forms. It is not impressive to have to ask for a pen, or to use a cheap plastic pen.

B. Résumés

This is a much-needed tool for securing an interview for a job. A résumé is your introduction on paper and sells you to the company before you arrive in person. It must therefore, communicate your best qualities. A résumé must be neatly typed, printed by a laser printer, or typeset at a print shop on high quality paper with no misspellings, no typographical errors, no smudges, and should not exceed two pages in length. Professional agencies can help you as can career services on campus. Several good books on résumés are at the library. Use them.

Be totally honest on your résumé. Do not exaggerate your experience, or lie about your education. The truth may not help you get the job, but a lie will lose it for you, along with your reputation. Do not attempt cleverness on your résumé to attract attention. It will likely come off poorly. Be direct and clear, state your assets with confidence, and dwell on the positive. Your cover letter should be on the same color stationery as your résumé. Be sure to include elected offices in your fraternal societies, positions of responsibility you've held, stating your accomplishments and achievements.

C. Business Lunches and Dinners

The biggest reason for business lunches and dinners is to get away from the distractions of the office, and get to know the people you are doing business with in a relaxed atmosphere. It has little to do with food, and everything to do with working relationships. Therefore, go to restaurants where you have been before, and know the food is good, service is great, atmosphere is quiet, and where you will be comfortable. If you are the guest, follow your host's lead as he takes you someplace where he is comfortable.

Ask your new peers to lunch, one by one, so that you will get to know them on a personal basis. This is also a great way to learn about the company. Be very modest about your past jobs and your qualifications for this new job. People are immediately attracted to someone who downplays his importance and usually thinks of that person as more important than he really is.

Every table has a "power chair," which faces the door or "audience" so the occupant can see everything that is going on. Give this seat to your guest.

Professional behavior is common sense and can advance your career. Whatever your position in business – whether you're an executive or someone who's just stepped onto the bottom rung of the corporate ladder – simple common sense consideration for others is always appropriate. It wins respect from others and marks you as a team player who is a real asset to the company, or if meeting with an alumnus, a real asset and ambassador for the chapter.

Be nice to everyone. Treat the people on the bottom of the job scale as well as you do the boss. If you are genuinely nice to everyone, you will improve the atmosphere and the office morale. Quite apart from the kindness and respect involved, these people will become your friends and valuable supporters, which will probably prove to be the greatest asset to your career.

Be **loyal** to and defend the boss inside and out of the office. Don't "rat" on anyone, unless that person is committing a serious offense (theft, drug using or dealing, losing customers, etc.). Unless you are a person's supervisor, don't criticize him or her directly, and especially not behind his or her back. After all, that person could be your boss one day. Don't put someone down and do not interrupt when you disagree with that person while making a presentation in the office, or before a customer. Voice your objections in private. To humiliate someone in public will not advance your career, and it is rude.

Always keep your promises. Establish – and keep – your reputation as that of a person of good faith. Pay back your lunch obligations. Don't become known as the person who never picks up the check.

Be nice to **newcomers**. Show them around, make them feel welcome and a part of the team. Give them a feel for the politics of the office. In other words, follow the Golden Rule, do the same for a newcomer as you would want done for you. When you're new in the office, you need information – on how things work, on what everyone does, on the politics of the office. You find out the answers to all those questions by asking intelligent questions of intelligent people when they have the time to talk to you. Timing is everything in the business world, and you must learn to be sensitive to it. Never take up someone's time when he or she is obviously late, on a deadline, or overloaded with work.

To find out how to approach customers and associates, review the files. This reveals how the people in the company write their letters, talk to their customers or clients, and communicate among themselves. Most important of all, listen! You are going to make more friends in two months by being interested in others, than in two years trying to get them interested in you. What you hear all around you is the best education of all. Some people, when they are new in an office, are so entranced by their own conversations that they hear nothing else. They are not listeners and thereby often lose the forest just to save a couple of trees.

To escape from a conversational dilemma, it is a good idea to bring up an entirely new subject of conversation. If a nasty argument has erupted, that's the time for a hero in the group to say something like, "Enough about that subject. What I want to know is who here is willing to make a wager on the outcome of the upcoming elections? Who knows who is ahead in the polls?" FOR FURTHER CONVERSATIONAL TIPS, SEE 2.I., page 16.

Good conversation is a pleasant – and kind – give and take of subjects of mutual interest. People weave in and out of it as spectators, listeners, and talkers. There are some people you always like to talk to – because they're upbeat, amusing or informative. These are people who make you feel relaxed, and who, when you run into them or join them in a business or social situation, cause a reflex reaction in your facial muscles – a nice big smile.

D. Men and Women at the Office

A man's behavior at the office is different from that off work. At work, he treats a female colleague as an equal and therefore <u>forgoes</u> typical social etiquette:

Don't:
- Open all doors for her
- Stand up when she enters the room unless she is a visitor
- Help her with her chair
- Serve her first at the table
- Have her precede when entering

- Help her with her coat when she arrives, or departs
- Walk curbside to protect her
- Light her cigarettes
- Order for her and always pay for meals

The polished professional treats people equally, according to acts of protocol – not gender – and either sex comes to the aid of the other, whoever needs assistance. For example:

Do:

- Move quickly to open a door for people with their hands full

- Stand to greet a visitor to the meeting, or the office

- Assist a colleague struggling to get in or out of a coat

- Pick up dropped items if it is more convenient for you to do so

- Let seniority precede through doors, male or female (a male president precedes a female vice president into rooms or when mounting platforms, etc.)

- Keep private lives totally separate from professional lives. If colleagues flirt with you, let them know that you do not appreciate the extra attention.

Additionally, keep in mind the following **professional attributes**:

- **Dress** is neat, clean, in good taste, appropriate for the job. There are regional differences for current business attire. In California, short-sleeves, open-necked shirts may be okay, but not on Wall Street or in the Northeast.

- **Grammar** is correct, speech is polite, without slang or profanity. The better the communication skills (proper, courteous, intelligent), the better the chance for promotion and advancement in the executive arena. Communication and technical expertise are a dynamic combination.

- **Positive attitude** will carry you far, emphasizing the good rather than the bad. If you bad mouth and challenge superiors, don't expect them to support you. "It is your attitude, more than your aptitude, that determines your altitude" goes an old saying. Smile.

- **Get to work on time**, meet deadlines, be prompt to meetings, and do not watch the clock to see if it is quitting time. If you are going to be delayed for any reason, tell the boss.

- **Use time well**, and avoid time wasters such as chatterers, meetings without an agenda, and unproductive tasks. Unless you have something important to discuss, leave busy superiors alone to work. **Respect the hierarchy**, the chain of command applies to everyone. If you leapfrog the hierarchy, and your immediate supervisor is caught unaware, you can be in trouble with both of them.

- **Keep business appointments**, and keep them short. Fifteen minutes is a good length of time, unless there is more both of you agree to discuss. The caller should make the first move to end the meeting.

- **Quality** and accuracy is vital. Errors cost money, even those of misspelling, faulty grammar, incoherent sentences, and wrong names. Customers can go elsewhere, and do.

- **Thoughtfulness and understanding** will improve the office dynamics. Avoid irritations, and awkwardness. Always use "please," "thank you," "good morning," and "good night." Be known as someone people want to work with.

- **Initiative** is welcomed. Look for things to do when you have extra time, ways to help others with their tasks, and help the company be more productive. This motivates others, and shows you have leadership potential.

- **Professionalism** leads to promotion. Be a professional every day, not just when the boss is looking, or a position is open.

Of course there are things to <u>avoid</u>:

- **Gossip** is deadly, and word will get back if you are repeating private matters given to you in confidence, or if you make critical remarks about the boss or co-workers. Assume your statements will be repeated.

- **Keep confidences** when you are privy to information on reports, unannounced plans, personal papers, etc. Remember that your salary, along with others, is confidential. Keep it that way.

- **Absences** should be avoided if at all possible. Just because you have sick days, does not mean you should take them. Your reputation should be one of sacrifice for the company, not working when it is convenient for you.

- **Personal problems** are to be left at home, even when your co-workers are your friends. Period. Share over lunch, but do not take company time to share or solve private matters.

- **Private phone conversations** should be restricted to only those that are urgent. Chatter about trivia is overheard, and those who believe in working will appropriately brand you a lightweight.

- **Do not waste time** with private visiting, wandering about, reading magazines, and talking to fellow workers. Keep at your work, or find some work to do. If you have time to waste, perhaps your job can be cut.

- Do not give yourself a **manicure** or style your hair at your desk. Do not chew **gum**. Do not prop your feet on the desk.

- **Friends and family** should not visit the office except on rare occasions. If you want them to see the new computer, visit on the weekends.

- **Sex and romance** have no place in the office. Sex with a colleague is almost always career suicide. Private and professional lives must be kept separate.

9. DRESS AND PERSONAL APPEARANCE

To be attractive, dress appropriately for social functions. It is impossible to talk about the right kind of attire without mentioning that the way you look depends not only on how you dress, but also on: your **posture and bearing** – the way you move in your clothes; or your **grooming** (without good grooming, nothing is fashionable or right). It is better to invest in a few quality things than many cheaper wardrobe items. Clothing made of good fabric with a good cut lasts for years. For example, if you amortize the cost of a good man's or woman's suit over a period of four years' wear, it is a real bargain!

A. Men's Professional Dress

A good wardrobe is adaptable. Lean towards the more traditional styles, which have become men's classics. This way you can survive fashion changes on a student and young professional's budget. Here are the **men's fashion classics** for a wardrobe:

Conservative suit dark navy, dark charcoal gray, or black; solids or soft stripes; all wool fabric, or wool-blend; single breasted, two or three pieced, with standard lapels. A solid dark blue is the first choice; almost everyone looks good in dark blue. Young professionals should build up to at least four suits to offer variety in your wardrobe.

Sports jacket in navy blue, wool or wool-blend, single breasted with gold buttons. **Slacks** for the blazer are gray or tan, wool or wool-blend, plain front or pleated.

Shirts are white, light blue, or subtle stripes; long-sleeved; Oxford or button-down collar; 100% cotton or cotton-blend Oxford cloth or broadcloth. Tab collars are okay.

Neckties complement the color of your suit or sports jacket – dark red, crimson, and burgundy ties always wear well; silk or silk-blend; subtle stripe, pin-dots, or small print. The tie makes the outfit, so be very choosy about the tie and ask for help in selecting ties if you are not color-conscious. Tie reaches the belt buckle when worn, and the knot has a dimple, if you can tie it that well. Bow-ties are best left for academia and tuxes.

Socks are black or dark navy, over the calf so the leg does not show when you sit down or cross your legs. **Shoes** are black or cordovan with dress laces, or loafers (with suit); or casual loafers (with sports jacket). Shoes are always polished. **Belt** color matches the shoes, if leather, and about one inch wide, with an understated buckle (don't draw attention to your waistline). **Suspenders** can add a nice touch to your outfit (match or coordinate with the tie), especially with pleated suit pants, helping them hang better. Avoid clip-ons. Wear a belt or suspenders, but not both. Carry a high quality pen. Wear a high quality wrist watch. Be careful to use cologne sparingly, not over-powering.

If you work for a conservative firm, dress as the other men do – conservatively. Save your avant-garde Italian styles for your weekends, and stick with the fashion classics. If you have a weight problem, dark-colored (blue, gray), single-breasted suits are best for you. Wear a lightweight dark suit in hot summer weather. A winter-weight fabric makes others feel hot by looking at it, not to mention what the wearer must be feeling. Brown suits are only for the fashion-secure, so stay away from them. Three-piece suits are the most conservative look of all. They wax and wane in popularity. Sometimes you see a lot of them; other times it seems they're going out of style.

If you're worried about what to wear on an informal weekend gathering, you can't go wrong with a dark blue blazer and gray wool slacks. Check with your host to see if you are supposed to wear a tie. A polo shirt or sweater looks great with slacks for a casual-dress event. A T-shirt does not. Never pair the top of a business suit with a pair of casual slacks. It doesn't work. Only a blazer or a sports jacket does the job for a casual look.

Men's fashion disasters. Watch your **socks** when you sit down. If there's a section of bare leg showing between the top of your socks and the bottom of your trousers, it's time for action – go to the store for some over-the-calf-length socks. Holes in your socks are another fashion faux pas. Combine the holey socks with scuffed-up shoes, and you're in real trouble. **Short-sleeved** business shirts worn without a jacket in the office look terrible in most people's opinion, even if they don't have the courage to admit it. When it's hot and you're jacketless, you can always roll up the sleeves of your long-sleeved shirt. White dress socks are: fine with an all-white summer suit; simply terrible with black or cordovan shoes and a suit; even worse when worn with black street shoes and shorts at a resort. Another disaster is a shirt that's too small, with pillows of fat bursting out between the buttons. Dandruff on the shoulders leaves a bad impression. Watch those loud plaids. Horses look good in plaid blankets, but...

If people tease you about your ties, let someone pick out your next ones for you. A tall man needs an extra-long tie; a heavy-set man needs a wide one. Wear your most conservative ties when your suits have a strong pattern or color; wear your bright or interestingly patterned ones with your most conservative dark suits. Pick up a color from your tie, or vice-versa, so there is instant color coordination. Avoid fat knots, and short ties that hang above the belt. (Ties should touch the belt.)

Jewelry. Less is more. A wristwatch, a gold signet ring, and a wedding ring are enough. More than one gold bracelet begins to be too conspicuous, and lots of gold chains lying in a jungle of chest hair, with the shirt proudly open at the neck to display it, is something most of us can live without viewing – permanently.

Shoes. Shoes should be highly polished and free of scuff marks. The heels of the shoe should be in good shape. Shoes, like neckties, should be the best you can afford. A great suit is ruined with either a poor tie or shoes. For the male professionals, two kind of leather shoes are acceptable at work – lace-ups and classic loafers. The colors men in authority wear are black, cordovan (mahogany) or dark brown.

In summary, well-dressed people dress properly for their job and their social life; buy clothes according to fashion, but also according to their figure and age; who have good powers of observation so that they can learn good taste from others who have it; who know how to look at themselves mercilessly in a full-length mirror before making a major purchase; and who would never ruin a terrific-looking outfit by a lapse in good posture or grooming. You may find all this difficult at first, but with practice it becomes instinctive, and then you'll hear yourself described as someone who really knows how to dress. Read the "dress for success" books for more details and tips.

B. Women's Professional Dress

Fashion has to fit your lifestyle, age, figure, and job. A well-dressed woman presents a total picture with her clothing, makeup, jewelry, and the way she carries herself. We all want to look, and feel, our best, and we know we are treated best when we look especially well. To do so, the right colors, fabrics, designs, and styles must match and balance body size, shape, facial features, and coloring. We choose the qualities we want to accentuate, and it is not a lie to stress the best. Creating a personal and professional style takes time, commitment, and a careful clothing budget.

Corporate women in the 1990s have made great strides away from the conventional "uniform." Women are freer to dress in ways that express individuality. However, it is still necessary and wise to dress conservatively in most professional settings.

For credibility, power, and to be considered a professional, wear a suit or jacketed dress. **Blazers** with a well-tailored dress are sharp. A **tailored suit** should be of top quality, excellent cut, and perfect fit. It needs to be cut for your body; never try to imitate a man's suit. The best colors are navy blue, black, red, mahogany, camel, and gray. Appropriate fabrics for the office are pure wool, wool blends, fine cotton, silk, and rayon. In a well-tailored suit with high heels or classic pumps, and a leather briefcase, the woman attorney is not going to be mistaken for a clerk when she shows up in court. The **skirt** is still regarded as the most professional attire for women, and should always be worn for special meetings and when you are making your best presentation. Well-tailored **pants or trousers** are practical on bitter-cold days, but as a new employee, don't be the first to wear pants. Be aware of subtle and not-so-subtle dress codes in the office.

A flair for fashion should not overshadow your professional skills. You can only sell one thing at a time, so avoid plunging "V" necklines, bare backs, see-through blouses, slit skirts, skirts way above the knee, and other clothing that is romantic or sexy and which draws attention to your physical attributes instead of your professionalism. These styles detract from your professionalism and will offend or alienate colleagues. Wear a bra, lest you draw attention you don't need.

Men's clothing "rights" and "wrongs" are much easier to understand. The range of clothing is limited for a man in a professional setting. For him, it's the quality that counts, and you can see it in the tailoring, the detail of the design, and the cut. You can distinguish the distinguished.

For women, there is so much choice and variety that it is confusing. Plus what looks great and "right" on one woman may not work for another, and send out a different message. To be treated as a professional and a leader, buy classic and quality clothes and accessories for your wardrobe. Add color and spice in small touches. Dress one step above where you are now. Buy clothing that is elegantly loose, rather than a little tight. A tight fitting outfit makes you look heavier and uncomfortable. Hose should always be worn in social or professional settings, even in the summer, no matter how good you think your tan is. The color of the hose should match your shoes or your dress, or both, for an integrated look.

Accessories should be <u>understated</u> and classic. They should enhance a wardrobe, but not draw undue attention or overpower. Hair, makeup, and hands are also accessories to your clothing. Hair is particularly noticeable. **Makeup** should be understated (i.e. very little) during the day, and slightly more for evening events when the lights are dim. Lipstick and eye shadow enhance the color of your skin and eyes in a nice way. Nails may be polished, but chipped nail polish should be repaired immediately. Nails should not be too long; two-inch "dragon lady" nails suggest you never have worked a day in your life. Never underestimate the importance of jewelry to finish an outfit. Simple and elegant is best; stay away from junk jewelry with a dime-store look. Perfume should be of high quality and remain extremely subtle, only noticed if immediately next to you. If someone starts to sneeze when you enter the room, take the message.

Integrate your entire outfit. If you need help, seek help from a friend or professional who has a flair for style and fashion. Read current books and magazines, and if need be, hire a consultant to help you put your wardrobe together for the professional look.

Leather Accessories.   Belts, shoes, and hand bags should be coordinated and complement each other in color for a unified look. Mahogany and black are traditional, but brown, burgundy, and patent leather work fine too.   The advice on leather accessories for men applies to women too. Don't carry shoulder bags made of cloth, denim, plastic, or raw leather. Large bags send out a poor message. Handbags should be small and plain, saying that the owner is organized. Leather attaché cases are appropriate for management level. Handbags should not rest on a desk or table during a meeting or meal. They should be stowed out of sight. If carrying a briefcase, use a small envelope purse that fits inside the briefcase. High heels are flattering, but not too high a heel. Classic pumps with medium height heels work for everyone and are best for work. A fairly narrow heel is most flattering to the leg. Shoes should be polished, and the heels should not be worn down. Boots may be worn to work, but not at work. Do not wear open sandals in the office.

Hats. Hats are an accessory to an outfit. A hat draws attention to you, and typically, improves posture and demeanor. Avoid large brimmed hats that obstruct eye contact. Old rules apply to hats. A woman may remove her hat while dining (men always do). A hat is removed in the office, and usually when calling on a client, removing it in the reception area. (See page 27.)

C. Informal Dress for Men and Women

Standards of dress vary from campus to campus. Neat, clean, and pressed is always in fashion, and good practice for the professional world. On a date, both should remember to be appropriately and nicely dressed for each other. People should make an effort to look clean and in fashion on a date – whether it's a dressy occasion or an informal get-together with friends. The theory is that the bigger the effort you make for a date, the more fun it will turn out to be (an old wives' tale that is mostly true!).

D. Badges and Letters

While in college, and at chapter events, it is expected that members will wear their insignia of membership when dressing up. Chapters differ, but as a guide, the Badge should be worn over or near the heart, whenever a coat is worn. For some, it may be also worn on conservative shirts or on a sweater. Badges should not be worn on athletic clothing, T-shirts, or other shirts without a collar. Principles of good taste and dignity are always kept as signs of respect. Some chapters have nice customs and traditions when a fraternity man offers his love his pin, in advance of engagement and marriage. She should wear his pin for dress-up only, and only when she also wears her badge, if in a sorority.

10. MULTI-CULTURAL AWARENESS

So much is changing in such a short time, it is difficult to keep up with social mores. We need to be alert to changes, and know how to handle them in today's terms. When you are in unfamiliar territory – geographically or culturally – observe those about you and when in doubt, ask, rather than risk an incident. Do your homework in advance, and try to be aware of the many subtleties and their importance.

A. International Business

The global economy is here to stay, and many corporations now have a presence world-wide in many foreign countries. You may have a chance to travel and do business around the world, and visitors from around the world will be at your door. Fortunately English is the world-wide language of business, with the exception of sections of East Asia, where it is Mandarin. However, there is a significant advantage in international business for those Americans who know at least one foreign language. No one is excused from not being worldly in dealing with people from other countries. People from other countries get upset that Americans don't bother to learn even a few basics of introduction and greeting, simply as a sign of respect. The Japanese, on the other hand, won't let an employee do business in the United States until a year is spent studying our customs and business practices.

International Blunders. Here are a few examples of international blunders that can harm a good relationship:

- Flashing the "OK" gesture to a Brazilian (that translates to our middle finger)

- Flashing the "V" sign to an Australian (that translates to our middle finger)

- Giving a clock to a visitor from China (symbol of death)

- Presenting a knife to a Japanese (symbol of suicide)

- Joking about "Montezuma's Revenge" to a Mexican

- Presenting a knife to a Latin American (symbol of cutting a relationship)

- Keeping your hands in your lap around Germans or Austrians (they are taught to keep their hands above the table at all times)

- Sending red roses to a German wife (red roses indicate a strong romantic interest)

- Telling a joke about the Queen of England to Canadians or the British

- Shaking hands with Asian women and children (disrespectful)

- Jumping to a first-name basis with the British, Europeans, or people from the Middle East

- Not studying a business card when presented by a Japanese

- Serving alcohol to a Muslim or Baptist

- Ignoring the strict dietary rules of Buddhists, Hindus, Jews, or Muslims (such as serving pork)

- Saying you're "stuffed" in New Zealand (relates to sexual intercourse)

- Wrapping gifts in white paper for a Korean or Japanese (color of death). Also, they don't use bows or brightly colored paper.

- Looking an American Indian elder in the eye (American Indians show respect by looking down). Also, some American Indians do not grip firmly during a handshake; doing so indicates aggressiveness.

- Serving foods common in America, which international visitors find unusual or even repulsive, such as corn-on-the-cob, crawfish, pumpkin pie, popcorn, white bread, grits, watermelon, hot dogs, and marshmallows.

- Likewise, repulsive to many Americans are delicacies of other lands, such as sushi (raw fish), dog meat, ant eggs, toasted grasshoppers, sheep's brains, raw monkey brains, slugs, stir-fried bees, sheep's eyeballs, and Scottish Haggis (sheep or calf innards).

Most blunders are innocent and inadvertent, but that does not excuse them. Cross-cultural training is important as it helps us work more effectively with people around the world, either temporarily or permanently. In diversity, there is an opportunity for more creativity, harmony, and more productivity. Being cosmopolitan creates value and profitability. Former United Nations Ambassador Andrew Young said, "We're running a $170 billion trade deficit essentially because the captains of American industry don't know how to deal with people who are different."

Cosmopolitan Skills. In approaching and working with people of different cultures, certain people skills help immensely even before learning the issues of protocol and etiquette. These are:

(1)   **Respect** for differences in cultures, customs, philosophies, speech, eye contact, body gestures, personal privacy, etc. You demonstrate your respect through acceptance, support, and encouragement for what is right and comfortable for them. Watch your host and follow his lead.

(2)   **Tolerance** for ambiguity and being able to react positively to new and different – if not unpredictable – situations. A cosmopolitan person quickly accepts Latin hugs, or Middle Easterners walking arm-in-arm with you in public, or eating food with your hands.

(3)   **Patience** is important as Americans are fast-paced and quick to get to business. Other cultures move with comparatively glacier-like slowness, and place a strong emphasis on getting to know each other first before business is approached.

(4)   **Empathy** means to put yourself in another person's shoes. Sense how difficult it may be for an international visitor to be in America, not understanding our customs and rules. Your sensitivity and understanding will be appreciated.

(5)   **Show interest** in new customs, religions, politics, foods, and culture that are new. Take an interest in others, and do not expect them to be Americans.

Research and planning is needed for dealing and meeting with anyone from a foreign country. Read up on the history, economy, politics, and customs of the country before meeting with someone. It is a compliment to the people you will be working with and will save you from embarrassment. Know your audience, and don't take yourself too seriously.

It is a natural inclination to take international guests to restaurants specializing in their national food: Chinese to an Oriental restaurant, Italians to the best Italian restaurant. Avoid doing this. The American version is usually not what they are accustomed to at home, and they want to experience and be acquainted with American cuisine. Ask their preference. If they are tired of strange meals, they might appreciate a taste resembling home. Be mindful that many people are vegetarians.

Canadians Are Not Americans. United States and Canada share the longest, least-guarded border in the world. Canada is the United States' largest trading partner representing over $200 billion in trade each year. The U.S. sells more to the Province of Ontario each year than to all of Japan. We trade more with the 27 million people of Canada than we do the 320 million people in the twelve countries of the European Community. The Free Trade Agreement signed between our two countries in January 1989 will create a near common market between the two nations in the next ten years. Canadians are Americans' best friends in many ways, and we have the friendliest border in the world.

How much do you know about Canada? Name four famous historic Canadian figures. Describe how Canadians are different. Who are Inuits? Describe the French influence. What are their major exports?

It is fair to say that we have a lot in common, but Canadians are not Americans. They have their own government, culture, customs, and heritage that is different than others.

Know and respect them. The same is true of Mexico and its people. Remember that Mexicans refer to people from the United States as North Americans. Also bear in mind when doing business in Mexico and in neighboring countries to the south, that their midday meal is the main one, eaten between 1 and 4 o'clock.

Mexicans are formal people and titles are important to them. You should refrain from using first names until invited to do so. As in other Latin countries, the attitude toward time is less rigid than among North Americans and a thirty-minute delay should not be a surprise. This is particularly common when hosting dinner guests in the evening.

B. Religions

Respect for other religions should guide your conduct. If you visit someone's place of worship, quiet, attentiveness, and dignity are appropriate. Smile and nod at people you know, and a whispered "hello" is okay. Do not visit until you are outside.

When you have an opportunity to visit a church or synagogue of a faith other than your own, do so. It is an enriching experience, and you will come away with more understanding of people whose beliefs are different from yours. Attending another service with an open mind will strengthen, rather than weaken, your values and beliefs. Read the service bulletin after you arrive to familiarize yourself. Follow the lead of the congregation. Stand when they stand, sing when they sing, pray when they pray. If there is a part in which you do not feel comfortable participating, just sit quietly until that portion of the service is done, keeping your integrity.

A non-member need not genuflect when entering a pew or make the sign of the cross in a Catholic or Episcopal Church. You do not have to kneel if your custom is to pray seated in the pew. Just bend forward and bow your head. If you feel more comfortable, however, do as others are doing. If you choose to sit when others are kneeling, lean slightly forward in consideration of the person behind you.

Usually you can take **communion** in a different church if you are baptized, but some churches do not permit non-members to receive communion unless confirmed in that church. Ask in advance. Watch what the congregation does and follow their lead. You will derive the same comfort and strength from the Host whether you receive it at the altar rail (Roman Catholics, Episcopalians, Lutherans), or if passed to you in the pew (Presbyterians). When attending church away from home, you should make a contribution when the offering plate is passed. It is a nice way of saying "thank you" to the church you are visiting.

Non-Jewish men keep their hats on in synagogues. There will be yarmulkes available for visitors without a hat.

C. Disabled

Treat the disabled like anyone else. With the exception of their disability, they are probably exactly like you. There are rules of etiquette that apply to disabled people, but by far the most important is <u>don't stare</u>, or draw attention to the fact they are different in any way. People getting about with wheelchairs, crutches, braces, mechanical arms, etc. take justified pride in their independence and approach to a normal life. The last thing they wish is to be reminded by curious or overly attentive persons that they have not achieved their goals. An offer of help to someone who must navigate a steep curb, get down a rail-less step, or get through a difficult door is always in order . . . just like you would with anyone else. But before you grab the wheelchair, ask politely if you can be of assistance.

Do not make personal remarks or ask personal questions of a person with a disability. Let them bring it up if they wish to talk about it. Never pry into their personal feelings or private matters. Do not "talk over" the disabled person or a person in a wheelchair. The attendant or spouse may be there to assist, but not speak for the disabled person (unless the disability is related to speech). If a co-worker has AIDS you can hug, squeeze, kiss, or shake hands with them, he can sneeze on you, and you can drink from the same cup. AIDS is not transmitted through these kinds of contact. Treat him with dignity and compassion.

With **deaf** people, their means of contact is visual. Be sure to include them in your group, and be sure they can see everyone. Speak distinctly and just a little slower. Do not use exaggerated mouth movements, as they have been taught to lip-read normal speech. If they are not facing you, a gentle tap on their arm or shoulder will get their attention. It is useless to shout. Be willing to repeat if necessary, and do not appear annoyed. It would only embarrass them and make understanding harder.

With **blind** people, their only disability is loss of sight. They have a problem to overcome that a sighted person does not, but most have learned to live like you with considerable success. When talking, use a normal voice and visit as you would with anyone else. No need to avoid the word "see," as they will use it as much as anyone. When entering a room with a blind person, make your presence known including using your name. Do not expect them to recognize your voice, unless you are a close friend. Let them know when you are leaving so they will not be left talking to the air. If offering assistance to blind people, never take their arm, let them take your arm which will give them more confidence. Do not attempt to play with the guide dog. Its attention must remain fully on the blind person, whose safety and well-being depends on their full attention.

Amputees and invalids should be treated like anyone else when greeting them. When you meet someone whose right arm is missing, extend your right hand even though he cannot shake hands in the usual way. He will take it with his left hand, and will feel more comfortable because you have made no unnatural gesture to accommodate his disability. If an artificial hand is offered, shake it as you ordinarily would, saying nothing and showing no surprise. If for some reason – arthritis, injury, or disability – it is painful to shake hands, that person will acknowledge your greetings and let you know it is painful to shake hands.

D. Other Lifestyles

Just as stereotyped marriages have been altered, so have stereotyped images of men and women in the world. With human understanding, polite society concentrates on our similarities as people, not our differences. We have come a long way to recognize that people are individually created, not stamped from a mold in the shape of the majority. Thus the disabled have been invited into mainstream society as have ethnic and religious minorities, mixed marriages, and gays. We have come to celebrate and value differences as the unique and diverse contributions all people can make to society.

Gays and lesbians are very much a part of our society today, and are an estimated five to ten percent of the population. Another significant percentage is bisexual. If you are not certain of someone's sexual orientation, do not ask what it is. Respect his or her privacy. If mutual acquaintances ask about their orientation, do not violate their privacy and answer, even if you know. Respond, "If you are curious about his private life, why don't you ask him?" That is how you would want someone to respond to a private question about you that you shared in confidence. It is not your place to "out" someone.

Remember that the most hurtful thing is to gossip about your homosexual friends or acquaintances just as it is inappropriate to share intimate details of your other friends. It only adds fuel to the fire of abuse that they already suffer at the hands of many people, and contributes to the emotional, psychological, and physical abuse they suffer. Discriminatory behavior against gays, lesbians, and bisexuals is not polite or thoughtful, and is against the law and ideals of a civilized society – the very ideals of democracy and freedom that America and the free world symbolize.

When two people of the same gender openly live with one another as partners in a monogamous relationship, they should be treated as a couple in every social sense. They should be invited to social functions as a couple, as you would other couples. The men should not be thought of as a safe date for a single woman friend, except as an escort for transportation purposes to and from the event as you would with another man.

When a gay or lesbian loses a companion, write a letter of condolence, send flowers to the funeral, and/or make a gift in memory of the deceased. Losing a partner is equal to the loss of a mate for a married couple. Treat gays with the same sensitivity.

Prejudice is a voice heard all too often – ethnic jokes, racial slurs, name calling, and sweeping generalizations. You should feel no need to laugh, or be silent, with such a display of poor taste. Quietly say, "I don't like comments (jokes) that belittle people," or simply get up and leave. If you are with friends of a minority group about whom the jokes or slurs are being made, your appropriate response to the slurs will speak volumes about you and your sensitivity. Change the conversation, or break away as soon as possible and apologize to your friends in private. If you are a member of the minority group, you can leave, be silent, or teach them a lesson that may temper their prejudice in the future. Just say "You must be talking about me." If they have any conscience at all, they will apologize.

11. HOSPITAL VISITS

For patients, hospital stays are shorter, which means that people in a hospital are truly ill or recuperating. Visits from family and friends can be comforting and heart-warming, but socializing needs to be limited because the patients are not up to it and need to conserve their energy to heal. Some people avoid seeing the sick, and miss an opportunity to be of service. Others fail to see the terminally ill and do not say goodbye or bring closure to an important relationship. Perhaps for some it is because a visit to the hospital is uncomfortable, and you do not know the rules of conduct.

Visitor rules vary from hospital to hospital, but here are guidelines that may help you feel more comfortable, as you offer comfort.

Check with family or friends before hand to see if the patient wants visitors, and if so, if they need anything delivered. Before going to the patient's room, check on the room number to be sure the patient has not moved, or someone reported it wrong to you.

Before entering the room, look above the door to see if the light is on. If it is, the patient is requesting help, so do not enter. Request help from the nurses' station. Respect a closed door. Check with the nurses' station to see if visitors are appropriate at this time. Observe signs on the door such as "no visitors," "do not disturb," "no smoking," or "isolation." Check with staff regarding any procedures you may not understand.

When entering the room, position yourself (standing or sitting) in the room for the patient's convenience. Be poised and calm when entering the room, not boisterous. Be natural. Shake hands only if the patient takes the initiative. Be mindful of oxygen, IV tubes, special equipment, etc. Be careful not to disturb any equipment or jar the patient's bed. If there are signs of discomfort or nausea, ask if you should return at a better time.

Keep your visit to five or ten minutes – no more unless asked to stay. Be a good listener, permitting the patient the freedom to share his thoughts and feelings. The purpose of your visit is to be comforting, not to be entertaining or social. If appropriate, bring plants, flowers, a small gift, the daily newspaper, favorite magazines, or reading material to cheer up the patient. Offer to run errands, or take care of matters that would take worries away. The staff attend to the needs of the patient, but do respond to requests for help not related to health care such as fetching items, watering flowers, reading cards, mailing letters, etc. Prepare to leave when the conversation lags or the patient looks tired. End the visit on a positive note, with words of assurance.

Give the **new mother** several hours before visiting (unless she is your wife!), and check with family first to see if she would like company. You may always see the new baby through the glass in the nursery. Give the parents a gift to mark the occasion, usually a gift especially for the baby such as a baby spoon, mug, rattle, picture frame, etc.

Do not probe into the patient's illness. If the patient does not volunteer that information, it is private and personal. Tell no one what is told to you in confidence. If staff come into the room to assist the patient, excuse yourself to wait in the hallway, or call your visit to an end. Do not diagnose the patient's sickness or offer cures. "I felt like you . . . and you know what it was . . . I bet you have . . . I took the same pills and they didn't help" are all statements of empathy, but are inappropriate and dangerous. Do not criticize the doctor or the treatments to the patient. Confidence in the doctor, hospital, and treatment are all important in them getting well. Do not worry the patient, or undermine the health care providers.

Do not visit if you have a cold or illness yourself. Sick persons are apt to be more susceptible to contagious diseases. Don't smoke in the hospital. Be cautious about wearing a strong perfume or cologne.

Do try to stay within the suggested **hours of visiting**. In most hospitals, visiting hours are fairly generous, especially for immediate family. The exception, of course, is for intensive care units where it makes sense to limit the length of time and the number of visitors. If a patient is scared, lonely, or worried about his situation, then it is the patient's right as a fragile human being to have visitors stay past visiting hours. Good friends accommodate such requests, but be mindful to inform the head nurse of the request.

If the patient is **terminally ill**, avoid the game of "everything is fine." Be willing to listen, and talk, about feelings of dying. Don't desert the dying patient, physically or emotionally. The healing part of your visit is that you care, and were willing to be there for them.

12. FUNERAL ETIQUETTE

Upon hearing of the death of an <u>intimate</u> friend, it is always appropriate to call the family home to offer friendship that the family might find helpful and comforting. This would entail a personal visit(s) to the family home, preparing food for the home, greeting other friends at the door, making telephone calls, sending of flowers to the home or funeral home, or the enclosure of a memorial offering. Offer the use of your car, and run special errands for the family should they need that service. Offer to care for small children of the deceased family, and also clean or watch the family home at the time the family might be gone to make funeral arrangements or be at the church for the funeral.

Other family friends should pay respects by going to the **funeral home** should there be a visitation, sign the guest register, and visit with the family. The newspaper notice will give details. This visit accords proper respect for the person who has died, and demonstrates a silent source of strength for the family. Telephoning is not improper, but it may cause inconvenience by tying up the line when they are trying to notify relatives and make arrangements.

The visit to the **funeral home** need not last more than ten minutes. As soon as you have expressed your sympathy to each member of the family, and spoken a moment or two with those you know well, you may leave. Your comments can be brief saying, "I'm so sorry" or "He was a wonderful person." If you were close, you can say, "We are going to miss John so much too." A brief embrace, a warm handshake, a few words of affection, your presence, and sympathy may be all that is needed. Do not ask about the illness or death unless the family brings it up first, and then only to listen and offer comfort and understanding.

If the casket is open, guests may pass by and pay respects to the deceased, and bow your head in quiet prayer. If it is difficult for you to do, you do not have to. Follow the religious customs of the family, but you do not need to do anything that is contrary to your own faith. For example, if there is a crucifix over the coffin of a Roman Catholic, Protestants need not cross themselves, and Jews need not kneel.

Attendance at a public **funeral** and/or memorial service is always important. Death is a lonely time for a family. Friends give them a feeling of support from their community. It is also nice to offer memorial contributions and/or flowers in memory of the deceased. Follow the wishes of the family with regard to memorials.

After the funeral, family and close friends go to the cemetery for the Committal Service. There may be no interment during the winter due to frozen ground. A reception will follow the interment, or immediately after the church service if there is not interment at the cemetery. Wait at the place of reception and await the family's arrival. Friends should go to the **fellowship** time after the service that is usually held at the place of the service. This gives the family time to visit with people and serves as a space where the family can express their appreciation to friends for their help and attendance at the service.

Wakes are customary for some ethnic groups and in some localities. On rare occasions, they are roaring festivities, with seeming gaiety. They are intended to be a celebration of their passage into eternal life and they help the family get their minds off the tragedy and loss. In most cases, a wake is a quiet luncheon or reception at the home of the family. Other people usually provide the food. This provides a meeting place and a meal for those who have come from out of town.

It is extremely important that friends keep in contact with the family after the funeral is held. Unfortunately, this is rarely done in our fast-paced society. Therefore, family is left alone with little support. Do keep in touch. Be available. Visits should be over a several week period of time. Invite the family to your home for lunch, dinner, or just a visit – to get them out of the house. Allow them to talk about the deceased. <u>Be a good listener</u>. This is the one thing the bereaved needs above all else. Say, "If you feel like talking, I'd like to listen." Accept silence. If the mourner doesn't feel like talking, don't force conversation. Be a friend to whom feelings can be confided and with whom tears can be shed.

There are also some things to avoid. They are:

Do <u>not</u>:

- Indicate death from a long illness is a blessing
- Indicate that a death is "God's will"
- Overstay your welcome at the family home
- Engage in visits of more than 5 minutes
- Begin a project to help a family without asking for permission from them
- Use trite phrases like, "This makes us feel terrible!" or "He is out of pain now."
- Talk about the deceased in the past tense
- Avoid using the deceased's name in conversation
- Use humor and levity. It is not appropriate.
- Be a busy body, intrude in funeral arrangements or give suggestions when not asked

A **card**, with **memorial to a charity**, should be brought to the viewing at the funeral home, or to the funeral service. The family preference for memorials is usually noted in the newspaper obituary or you can call the funeral home. The card should be addressed simply "The Funeral of Mary Louise Smith" or "To the Family of Mary Louise Smith." The envelope should contain your name and mailing address with a simple handwritten statement such as, "With deepest sympathy from the brothers of Sigma Alpha Epsilon." You might write a letter of condolence sharing some of your own remembrances about the person who died describing memorable incidents. Use everyday language and avoid flowery prose. "I remember the wonderful conversations we shared over coffee," or "John really helped me with my basketball game, and his coaching on . . .," <u>not</u> "Our heartfelt sympathy goes out to you in this hour of need," or "Our deepest sympathy goes out to you." Use your note to remember the good times and express your words of comfort.

Flowers may also be sent to the funeral home, or to the church according to the family's wishes. Flowers are not sent to Orthodox Jewish funerals, and sometimes only the family has flowers at Catholic funerals. Check with the funeral home to be sure what may be appropriate.

Pallbearers. Friends and relatives of the deceased are asked by the family to serve as pallbearers and ushers at church funeral services. Traditionally men have been asked, but today women are being asked too. It is a distinct honor to be asked by the family of the deceased to be an <u>honorary</u> pallbearer. It is an honor one does not refuse unless there is a exceptionally good reason. Men wear dark suits, white shirts, conservative dark tie, black shoes and socks. Women dress in subdued dark suits or dresses of solid color, simple and conservative.

In Christian funerals, six to ten pallbearers, in pairs, escort the casket, and they sit in the front pews, opposite the family. Honorary pallbearers follow pallbearers. The funeral home personnel direct the handling of the casket, and will brief you on what to do.

Jewish Services. Orthodox, Conservative, and Reform Jews have different customs for funeral services. When a Jewish friend dies, it is appropriate to bring or send a basket of fruit to the family, or bring gifts of food, as mourners are not permitted to do any work during this time of mourning. If the family is Orthodox Jews, they will be at home "sitting shivah," observing the seven-day period of mourning during which families honor their departed loved ones. They do not have any contact with the outside world, do not take phone calls, or conduct business. Every evening, close friends may come to the home to participate in a religious service. One should bring kosher food if the family is known to observe those dietary laws, or if one does not know the religious practices of the family.

Crying is a means by which people work their way out of grief and loss. Tears are not evidence of weakness. Weeping can be a shared experience. You can also laugh with your friends, enjoying memories and recounting humorous times. Death need not put a ban on laughter, just frivolity. Touching can be a comforting way to communicate when words are not enough or meaningless. Your presence and a squeeze of the hand, or an embrace, can eloquently tell them how much you care.

During mourning, encourage the postponement of major decisions. In time, gently draw the mourner into quiet outside activity. When they return to social activity, be as normal as possible. Be aware of their need to progress through grief. Remember that holidays, birthdays, and anniversaries may be especially difficult for the bereaved. Call them on that special day just to tell them you are thinking of them. Invite them to share the day with you. Understand they may need to express their grief for months. Healing is a long process. There is no need to pretend that life goes on just the same as it did before their loved one died. Rather than ask if they need anything, to which they will likely respond with a polite "no," do telephone them and visit, drop by with food, take the children out to events, invite the family to your home. Demonstrate that you care and you have not forgotten them.

AFTERWORD

This book is for you. Hopefully, reading these pages has given you insight, assistance, information, and support – even given you confidence that you have been doing the right things. We know that you will not only be judged for your knowledge and ability, but also your polish and professionalism, your manners at work and in your social life, and as an American, you will be an ambassador as you travel away from home. Again, we would like to thank Letitia Baldrige for allowing us to utilize her expertise and good works in preparing this publication.

Remember: the true test of good manners is the ability to tolerate bad manners. Never use your knowledge of manners, etiquette, and protocol to put someone else down. You would not be kind and thoughtful, which is the first rule of good manners. Not only observe the rules of conduct, but the spirit behind them.

Likewise, know that you will make mistakes, probably in high places. We have all been embarrassed, even mortified, by our own faux pas. We survive these gaffes, pick ourselves up off the figurative floor, and carry on resolved to do better the next time. Being able to laugh at yourself shows class.

Acquiring tact, diplomacy and manners will help set the tone for good relations wherever you go. Everyone can be smooth at work, perform flawlessly, with confidence in every situation . . . with a little practice. Good manners are part of working smart, as they are cost-effective, increasing customer service, contributing to employee morale, improving the company image, and playing a role in increasing profits. Customers and employees hunger for such high-class treatment.

Good manners mean good business, and good character, too.

Good breeding is the result of much good sense,
some good nature, and a little self-denial for the sake of others,
and with a view to obtain the same indulgence from them.

– Chesterfield

TEST YOUR "EQ" - ETIQUETTE QUOTIENT

Social Introductions (Pages 1-6)

1. How do you introduce your girlfriend to the chapter president?
2. Is it okay to leave an event to call a friend?
3. Does your hand go up and down when you shake hands?
4. Do you rise when someone new enters the room?
5. How do you receive an alumnus or guest of honor?
6. Who gives a toast when there is a guest of honor?
7. When do you start using the first name of an elder?
8. When do you use "Miss" as a title?

Table Etiquette (Pages 6-20)

9. Diagram a formal table setting with dessert spoon.
10. Do butter plates and salad plates go to the right?
11. Should salt and pepper shakers be passed separately?
12. Do women precede men into the dining room?
13. Where do guests sit?
14. When do you place a napkin on your lap?
15. Where do you place a napkin after the meal?
16. In what direction do you move the soup spoon?
17. How do you butter, and eat, bread and rolls?
18. What is the rule for using utensils in the correct order?
19. Name a couple of common table etiquette "faux pas."
20. Where do you place a spoon after you use it?
21. Where do you place an olive pit after you remove it?
22. When you are done eating, where do your knife and fork go?
23. When can you put your elbows on the table?
24. How many pieces of food should be cut at a time?
25. How do you hold a knife when cutting?
26. What is the difference between American and European styles of cutting meat and eating?
27. Where do you find the dessert spoon and/or fork during a prearranged setting?
28. Is it appropriate to stand when your date leaves the table?
29. Is it okay for you to push food on your fork with a piece of bread?
30. Food is served from the left or right?
31. What is the greatest sin of table conversation?
32. Where can you use a toothpick?
33. How much should you tip in a modest restaurant?

Telephone Etiquette (Pages 21-23)

34. How do callers get an impression of you from whomever answers the phone?
35. The phone should be answered in how many rings?
36. Is it okay to keep a caller on hold?
37. What are the elements of a good message?
38. How should you identify yourself on the phone?
39. Between what hours is it proper to call?
40. When answering someone else's phone, what should you say?

Social Functions (Pages 24-31)

41. What are the essentials of planning a party?
42. How would you be a thoughtful guest?
43. When do you rise for others?
44. When do you remove your hat and gloves?
45. When do you offer someone an arm?
46. Who always gets preferential treatment when opening doors?
47. Who goes through a revolving door first?
48. How does a lady get into a car or taxi?
49. When does a woman indicate she will split the check?
50. When during a meal is a good time to sing?
51. What are the basics of a good thank-you note?
52. When do you apologize?
53. When do you send a letter of apology?

Self-Protection from Social Abuse (Pages 31-36)

54. How many drinks are appropriate before a meal? During? After?
55. What do you do when a steward brings your table the wine?
56. How do you handle drunks?
57. How should a woman, or man, avoid date rape?
58. If you have doubts about your partner's sexual desires, what should you do?
59. Is alcohol a good excuse for pushing for sex?
60. When should you use a condom?
61. How do you handle unwanted, repeated sexual attention?
62. What do you do if sexual harassment persists?

Public Conduct (Pages 36-42)

63. What are your responsibilities as a campus citizen?
64. How do you handle sandbox politics?
65. What is the rule of 5% in philanthropy?
66. What three things can you offer to charity?
67. How do you voice criticisms to a waiter?
68. When is it appropriate to praise a waiter?
69. How do you show deference to the elderly?
70. How should you dress when traveling?
71. Do you face the flag or the music during the National Anthem?
72. When you display the flag near a podium, where does it go?

Correspondence (Pages 42-45)

73. What are the basics of writing a good letter?
74. Can you type a personal letter?
75. How do you check someone's title before writing?
76. When do you use the title "Ms."?
77. How do you address the envelope to a couple living together, but not married?
78. What are some negatives to watch out for in letter writing?
79. What does RSVP mean?
80. What does "regrets only" mean?
81. Within what time should you send a thank-you note?
82. Do you take people to lunch when you are new at a job?

Professional Etiquette (Pages 46-52)

83. Where do you find out about a company you are interested in?
84. How do you find out the name of the interviewer?
85. How do you dress for an interview?
86. Where do you sit in an interview?
87. Do you shake hands with the interviewer?
88. Is a résumé your introduction on paper?
89. What is the biggest reason for a business lunch?
90. How do you be nice to newcomers?
91. How does a man's behavior with women differ at the office?
92. What are some good personal attributes?
93. What kind of behavior should you avoid at the office?
94. Should you talk about private problems with your friends at the office?

Dress and Personal Appearance (Pages 52-56)

95. What is the best color suit to wear?
96. What are the best color neckties?
97. What color and kind of shoes are best with a suit?
98. What color should a blazer be?
99. What color socks should you wear?
100. Do you buy short-sleeve shirts for work?
101. What is the best fabric for suits?
102. List some men's fashion disasters.
103. Should you accent your outfit with lots of jewelry?
104. When should a woman wear a suit?
105. What are good colors for women's suits?
106. When is it practical for women to wear pants?
107. What fashions should be avoided in the office?
108. How much make-up is appropriate?
109. What shoes are best for office wear?

Multi-Cultural Awareness (Pages 57-62)

110. What are some examples of international blunders?
111. What are some good cosmopolitan skills?
112. Should a Protestant make the sign of the cross at a Catholic Mass?
113. Do you take communion when visiting a church?
114. Do you greet and visit with someone whom you know in church?
115. How do you greet a disabled person?
116. What do you do when you leave the room with a blind person?
117. How do you get the attention of a deaf person?
118. How do you shake hands with an amputee?
119. How do you respond if someone asks if a friend is gay?
120. Do you invite gay partners as a couple?
121. What do you say if someone makes a racial slur in front of your friend of that minority?

Hospital Visits (Pages 63-64)

122. How long should your hospital visits be?
123. How do you offer comfort to the patient?
124. What are appropriate gifts for new parents?
125. Should you visit a hospital patient when you have a cold?

Funeral Etiquette (Pages 64-67)

126. What do _intimate_ friends do for the family of the deceased friend?
127. How do family friends pay respects?
128. What is a wake?
129. What do you say to the bereaved?
130. Do you let the bereaved talk about the deceased?
131. What are some things to avoid at funerals?
132. What should pallbearers wear?
133. How should you respond to the death of a Jewish friend?

Enclosed is my order for <u>"Pardon Me, Your Manners Are Showing!"</u>

1-5 copies   @ $10 each, plus $3 shipping and handling
6-20 copies   @ $8 each, plus $5 shipping and handling
21 or more copies   @ $7 each, plus $8 shipping and handling

Please send:

_____ copies at $_____ per copy = $ _____

Plus shipping and handling $ _____

Total amount enclosed $ _____

(Payable to the Center for Innovation & Business Development)

All orders must be prepaid (purchase orders accepted).

Ship to: _____
             Name

             _____
             Organization

             _____
             Address

             _____
             City, State, ZIP

             (_____)_____
             Telephone

Mail to: "Pardon Me" Book
             Center for Innovation
             Box 8103, UND Station
             Grand Forks, ND   58202

Enclosed is my order for "Pardon Me, Your Manners Are Showing!

1-5 copies   @ $10 each, plus $3 shipping and handling
6-20 copies   @ $8 each, plus $5 shipping and handling
21 or more copies   @ $7 each, plus $8 shipping and handling

Please send:

_____ copies at $_____ per copy = $ _____

Plus shipping and handling $ _____ _____

Total amount enclosed $ _____

(Payable to the Center for Innovation & Business Development)

All orders must be prepaid (purchase orders accepted).

Ship to: _____
             Name

             _____
             Organization

             _____
             Address

             _____
             City, State, ZIP

             (_____)_____
             Telephone

Mail to: "Pardon Me" Book
              Center for Innovation
              Box 8103, UND Station
              Grand Forks, ND   58202